What the Media

"Refreshing to see a book, which instincts, straight from the heart manner the book conveys a simple mantra; to motivate yourself and others. Dotted with real life examples, the book is inspirational and motivates people. It enables the reader to draw on his own strengths and weaknesses making it even more personal.

Business India

"This book lets rhyme rule reason." It soft sells Emotional Intelligence and, it makes one think.

Business Today

"Win-Win Situation." *Heart over Matter* addresses the power of personal motivation and really offers a new mantra for success. Heart has its reasons which reason doesn't understand.

Economic Times

"This book catches the right pulse of the reader." That is why it went for reprint within 20 days of its arrival in the market. Emotional competency has been discussed and delineated in detail. *"The book comes as a whiff of fresh air"* as it lays stress on integrity and righteousness in one's life and value based leadership.

Times of India

It's a serious book and a New Mantra For Success. The Author attempts to answer many questions.

Hindustan Times

"A book that makes you think." Though he calls it a "motivation self-help book", there is enough in it to make one ask oneself some hard questions about what he/she has done with his/her life. A must read for all, as everyone would identify with the book.

The Hindu

The book can alter the mind set of people as well as bring about a positive change.

The Week

"Fresh look at Emotions, Motivation and Success." Unique inclusion of small questionnaires help the reader to identify his/her traits better. Simple and lucid language.

Indian Express

Here is a refreshing solution, for success and satisfaction. Delayed gratification and Perseverance and not shortcuts will get you success. The book, considered India's answer to "Dale Carnegie books "on personality development is set to be translated in Kannada shortly.

Vijay Times

This book combines motivation and Emotional Intelligence – two key factors, for success. *"A book that looks at success holistically."* It also deals with value based leadership and motivation.

Deccan Herald

It is divided into 8 chapters, each bearing a stamp of *"unmistakable originality and visionary"*. He presents extensive references and mind blowing illustrations, making the book a veritable guide for success – a thoroughly realistic approach. This book has immense potentials to be treated as a *"true masterpiece'*. Invaluable asset for generations of people to follow in all parts of the world.

Competition Success Review

This book has tips on organisational culture, human performance and motivation – the three critical areas that make or mar a company. *"This is being compared with the world's most popular books on motivation by Dale Carnegie and not without a reason."*

Voice and Data

Heart Over Matter is a guide that encompasses tips for **"more profitable work and better interpersonal relationships"**. Main thrust is on how to be a better human being, co-worker and a leader. Easy to understand, it is a comprehensive guide to finding own success. Exercises help the reader to get involved.

Asian Age

Success is a Serious Business . . .

"You don't fool around and become successful, but when you are successful, don't fool around."

© Virender Kapoor 2004

Read on....

Testimonial

It was a pleasure going through your book. I must say that it is a thought provoking, action inducing book which is easily understandable and refreshingly different. The book honestly delves into the tender resources of the heart and is a direct road map to success brought about in a very simple and lucid manner with examples and instances that one can easily relate to.

It is a must read book for everyone in the corporate world – from a junior executive to the top echelons of the executive ladder. In fact, it is equally relevant to people from all walks of life, be it a professional, student, or even a housewife. It will improve their careers, businesses, health and marriages. This wonderful book is an asset to any person, who applies its lessons – **"A must read for everyone".**

Ex Chief Vigilance Commissioner   **N. Vittal (IAS)**

Heart
MIND
OVER
MATTER

*"You can take a horse to the water and make him drink,
but if you take an ass to the water you can't make him drink."*

A new Mantra for success

Heart MIND OVER MATTER

YOUR MANTRA FOR SUCCESS

SECOND EDITION

Virender Kapoor

MACMILLAN

First Published 2004
Reprinted 2004-2008 (Eight Times)
Second Edition 2011

MACMILLAN PUBLISHERS INDIA LTD
Delhi Bangalore Chennai Kolkata Mumbai
Ahmedabad Bhopal Chandigarh Coimbatore Cuttack
Guwahati Hubli Hyderabad Jaipur Lucknow Madurai
Nagpur Patna Pune Raipur Thiruvananthapuram Visakhapatnam

Companies and representatives throughout the world

ISBN 10: 0230-32270-0
ISBN 13: 978-0230-32270-7

Published by Rajiv Beri for Macmillan Publishers India Ltd
2/10 Ansari Road Daryaganj, New Delhi 110 002

Typeset by Arpit Printographers
arpitprinto@yahoo.com

Printed at Sanat Printers
312 EPIP, Kundli, Sonipat 131 028

Preface to the Second Edition

After a spectacular success of *Heart over Matter*, in English, which is in print for several years, the book is now available in several regional languages like Hindi, Marathi, Gujarati, Malayalam, etc. Acknowledging its relevance and its wider readership among students, housewives, senior executives, top Business Schools and CEOs, I wish to broaden the scope of this book and take it to an altogether different level. I wish to experiment with a 'new dimension' which has never been used till now in 'Self help books.'

Since the book has Emotional Intelligence (EI) and motivation at its core, I all along knew that the subject does not fall into a 'Quantifiable Domain'. There is much more to EI than meets the eye. We are similar to each other as human beings but yet so different. Isn't it surprising that out of billions of people on this planet no two finger prints are the same! Similarly, our emotional acumen or nuances also hugely differ from one another.

While looking at the characteristics of individuals one would be surprised to note that no sun sign description says that people born under a particular sun sign are great at Physics or have a very high IQ. There may be some hunch in this regard but largely the description matches or describes your "Other abilities" like creativity, emotional sensitivity, impatience, will power, optimism, sense of humour, being impulsive, friendly nature, cool temperament and so on.

I, therefore, identified a startling resemblance between Emotional Intelligence and what characterization is described for each sun sign. After examining this in detail and trying to correlate it with the domains of EI, I found a very good connect. In the domain of EI – as you will realize when you finish reading this book – it is almost impossible to quantify things accurately. You could say "I am creative" but won't be able to say "I am 8 on a scale of 10 as far as creativity is concerned" – which itself is an approximation.

Having said so, I intuitively included the astrological dimension to this book. When I discussed it with Mr. Sanjay Singh, the Chief Publisher of Macmillan Publishers India Ltd., the idea was accepted immediately as "revolutionary but workable."

This book is about human success and explores deeper into those areas which are not often very well defined.

Virender Kapoor

Preface to the First Edition

Every individual wants to be successful and it is largely accepted that motivation is the key to one's success. Not surprisingly, therefore, there are a large number of books on motivation and success.

A number of recent studies also indicate that Emotional Intelligence (EI) is yet another key to success. EI is that area of human abilities, which plays a much bigger role than any other (life) skill, in making a person successful. EI consists of simple things such as caring for others, managing your moods, loving your job, handling impulse or even, simply getting along with people. These qualities are more important than being, say for example, a great mathematician or a top-class engineer. These traits on the 'emotional plane' make top performers (of people) in any professional area.

Literature on EI may not necessarily focus on motivation and success, whereas books on motivation and success do not often take into account the emotional factors that mould people and situations. I have made a sincere attempt to bridge that gap by bringing these two important elements together. Books on motivation generally talk about the mechanism of motivation and take the systematic, 'going-through-the-motions' approach. Motivation, morale and success, I, feel, are far more deep-rooted and have more to do with chemistry, than physics. Here actions and reactions come straight from the heart. It is difficult, if not impossible, to mug up a dozen points, repeat them twice a day and keep yourself motivated! To motivate your own self and others, you need to be in touch with your heart!

In fact, emotions, motivations and success are very closely linked and I presume, one cannot exist without the others. Without emotional arousal, you cannot be motivated and without motivation, you cannot perform. Without performing, you cannot be successful! I have aligned emotions, attitudes and motivation and strung them through a common thread to show how human abilities can be optimised to achieve spectacular success. I have, therefore, used EI and emotional abilities as the framework for this book, but have kept motivation and success in the forefront, as the thrust areas. Emotions come straight from the heart and *that is* at the heart of this book. I have kept my ideas and analyses simple, straight-from-the-heart and downright practical. A reader can relate it to his or her life, environment and most importantly, use these principles to attain success. This book, therefore, has the fabric of emotions and the complexion of motivation, passions, success and satisfaction, making for a unique reading experience. This book is for every one – students, professors, home-makers, engineers, doctors, managers, top executives. It is also for all those who are happily employed and the unemployed. It will surely appeal to all age groups.

Without emotions, it is often said, you can manage but you cannot lead. This book also conveys that without emotions, you can (strive) survive but cannot (survive) live! This is about heart over matter – read on.

Virender Kapoor

Acknowledgements

Every author needs encouragement, assistance and help from others to put his thoughts together and write a book – I am no different.

I want to thank my wife, Laxmi, for giving apt suggestions, painstakingly going through the manuscript several times and discussing incidents, anecdotes and stories that are narrated in this book.

I also want to thank my son Samir for suggesting such an appropriate title for this book. I feel, I could never have come up with such a suitable one on my own.

I wish to thank Mr Kishor A Chaukar, Managing Director, Tata Industries Limited, Mr Vivek Vyavaharkar, CTO, Bharti Airtel and Mr Ram Kumar, Head, HR HSBC Software Development Global Technology Center for reading the manuscript and for all their encouragement and valuable views on the subject.

Many thanks to all my friends and well-wishers who helped me in more than one way to get this book going.

I would like to thank Fluffy, our family dog, who taught us what unconditional love, is and in a way brought us closer together as a family. In today's world, you cannot expect such commitment and love from human beings – not even a fraction of it. This book is about caring, commitment, emotions and relationships, and we have learnt a lot about these from Fluffy.

I also want to thank God, who gave me the opportunity to meet so many good people from whom I could learn and pick up good habits and human values that go into the making a genuine human being.

Virender Kapoor

Introduction

'The line between failure and success is so fine that we scarcely know when we pass it; so fine that we are often on the line and do not know it.'

– Elbert Hubbard

WHAT IS THIS BOOK ABOUT?

This book is about emotions, attitudes, motivation, satisfaction and success. With Emotional Intelligence as the backdrop, it addresses those basic human instincts that are important for our success and satisfaction. Studies now show, that these very qualities make great leaders of people in all walks of life. It has a flavour of practicality, which you will be able to relate to in your day-to-day life. Instead of treating Emotional Intelligence in a very cut-and-dry manner, I have put it across in a more practical, light-weight, and humorous way, without diluting the essence of the subject. It will make you ponder over your own strengths and weaknesses. It would further, urge you to work on your positives and leverage them to your advantage. While identifying your strengths and working on them, you could reach the critical mass of good habits, that are so crucial for success. It will also encourage you towards making serious efforts to identify your negatives and work on them. Remember, change is possible in each one of us and it can happen at any age. This book will help you bring about that change. This book is more about satisfaction than success, because satisfaction is the greatest success. If this point is understood clearly, success in all other forms will follow.

> In the United States, an eminent judge was travelling in a train. When the ticket checker came, the elderly judge could not find his ticket. According to the procedure, the ticket checker summoned the inspector to fine the passenger. The Inspector recognised the judge who was still searching his pockets for his ticket and said, 'Sir, I am sure you are carrying your ticket, so don't bother to look for it now.' The old judge replied, 'I am not looking for the ticket to show it to you. I am looking for it because I have forgotten my destination!'

Like the judge forgot his destination, we also seem to have lost ours. We don't know where we are going as a society or as individuals. This book will help you find your own destination and give you right direction.

This work is also about our minds and mindsets. We have good minds, but need to change our mindsets. A good mind with the wrong mindset will not get you anywhere. This realisation will help you change your mindset. I have personally, gone through good and bad times like anyone else, and I am emotionally as vulnerable as anyone else.

I had my sorrows and joys, victories and defeats. Therefore, I have shared my experiences wherever appropriate. In my own life, I have trusted people, and more than 95 per cent of the times nobody has ever let me down – they reciprocated my trust. Five per cent of bad experiences don't stop me from trusting people. This book will help build trust – between people and within organisations.

In today's turbulent times, we need a balance between the heart and the head – an appropriate response to situations and people. This book is about interpersonal skills – handling people. It boils down to emotional optimisation, which is at the very core of this book. I have used those basic time-tested principles, that have been used since ages by great men and women as their guiding principles. These are universal in nature and are applicable to all.

'Only the wisest and the stupidest men never change.'
– Confucius

WHO SHOULD READ THIS BOOK?

This book is for those who want to bring about a positive change within themselves. Remember, no one can change you, if you don't want to change. Wives cannot bring about a change in their husbands, bosses can't change subordinates, subordinates can never change their bosses and friends give up trying to change their friends. Change has to start from within. Books can inspire, but not motivate you. Motivation implies moving yourself and that, you have to do yourself, nobody can do it for you. Each one of us has a different ignition level.

Take three balls of cotton, sprinkle petrol on one of them,

kerosene on the other and mustard oil on the third and try to light them separately with a matchbox. The cottonball doused in petrol, catches fire the fastest, and the most difficult one to set fire to, is the mustard oil cotton-ball. If you are the 'mustard oil' variety, then be prepared to dig harder – you may hit petrol somewhere deep down. This would require a genuine effort on your part. The positive side of it is that mustard oil once lit, lasts for quite sometime. In the overall context, each one of us has lots of good points. Only 15 to 20 per cent of weaknesses or shortcomings need to be handled. These shortcomings differ from one person to another. Some of us, for example, can make friends easily, but have a problem with our temper. Some people have a cool temperament, but are insensitive to others. Handling these shortcomings is like fine-tuning your engine for better performance. This book is also for those who want to know the key areas of strengths of people who have been great leaders, respected mentors and successful human beings.

HOW TO READ THIS BOOK

You need to read this book seriously, because it will bring a valuable change in you. It will change the way you look at things, situations and people. It will act as a battery charger and bring that 'feel good' factor in you through emotional literacy. It will do magic to your interpersonal skills at home, in your social circle and at your workplace. It will motivate your heart forever. So, keep this as a personal reference book on which you can build your life in a more meaningful way.

You could, while reading, underline the points that are

most relevant to you. Consolidate these after you have finished a chapter. At the end of each chapter, I have summarised the main points covered, in a nutshell. This will help you consolidate the gains. I .have also given a few questions and a few important points at the end of each chapter. Make a serious effort to read them and write down the answers honestly. It will do a lot of good to you and will define your personal road map for success and satisfaction.

At the end of the book, there are some simple questions so that you may evaluate yourself on some major and very important parameters. Make sure that you attempt this. This will be an eye-opener, as far as your own strengths and weaknesses are concerned. You will be surprised to see how strong you are. Use this to assess and evaluate yourself and work on your drawbacks for a happy and successful life. Most importantly, pass these things onto your colleagues, friends, subordinates and children at home. For maximum benefits, let the kids read this at home.

Like we take care of personal hygiene, take these things as an exercise in achieving emotional sanitation. Practice all that you learnt regularly and use it frequently on a day-to-day basis and I guarantee you change – which will change your life.

Virender Kapoor

'It is always morning somewhere in the world.'
– Richard Henry Home

Contents

1

New Benchmark
for Success:

There is more than What
Meets the Eye

*'The heart has its reasons which reason does not
understand.'*

– Blaise Pascal (1623–62)

WHAT IS HAPPENING TO US TODAY AS A
SOCIETY?

In the last five decades or so, we have made tremendous
economic and technological advancements – may be
much more than that what we achieved in the last 5,000

years. We have, with equal rapidity suffered societal decay, where most indicators of ill-being and unhappiness, such as being lonely, divorce and suicides are widespread, and are on the rise. It is not confined anymore, to the western economically advanced countries, as the same phenomenon is now clearly visible in the developing nations too. These developments act like a centrifugal force, keeping us away from one another in terms of personal relationships, family bonds as well as collective well-being and capacity for collective action as a society. Interpersonal relations are at their worst, although there is a lot of noise and hullabaloo about interpersonal skills.

The economic capital has increased but social wealth has ebbed to its lowest level ever. We have doubled our incomes in the last few decades and tripled the buying power of our money. We have better houses, more to eat, faster communication and our life expectancy has gone up from 47 years in the twentieth century to 76 years in the twenty-first century.

However, as mentioned before, our social wealth has depleted. Since 1960, divorce rates have doubled in the western world, violent crimes have quadrupled and depression and psychic disorders have soared to ten times the number. Developing nations are fast catching up. More rage runs in our blood than ever before. There is no tolerance, patience and no resilience left in us anymore.

There is, today, a lack of social commitment. The number of people joining local organisations like boy scouts and neighbourhood associations has reduced over the years and there are very few volunteers ready to devote

themselves to a social cause. Most civic organisations in general, are experiencing a decline in membership over the last decades. *When a group of neighbours informally keep an eye on one another's homes – that's social wealth in action.* Today, we don't even know who all our neighbours are.

People joined the armed forces for honour, valour, patriotism and commitment to a cause. Across the world, armed forces have thrived on *espirit de corps* and *raison d'être*, having a strongly embedded value system and traditions. Today, most economically developed nations have no takers for the armed forces, that have also taken a beating in the wake of economic boom and depletion of our social wealth.

Today, attending to religious duties, like church-related services, *Kar Seva, Guru Ka Langar*, etc., are considered old-fashioned rituals. Participation is thus, on the decline. Solo spirituality, is preferred to communal religion.

More marriages today, are being rocked than ever before. Divorce is no more only for people from the West. Young married couples, in the orient, and the Occident, are struck by the incompatibility syndrome. A young married couple nowadays, is ready to claim at the drop of a hat, 'We are not compatible.'

Remember, only plugs and sockets are compatible – humans learn from, grow with and live with each other. They co-exist. We have become too 'matter-of-fact' in our approach towards relationships.

This is also an era of corporate cold war, with restructuring,

downsizing and change management becoming the latest *mantras* for survival in the competive market. Pressures at work and home put people on a short fuse. *We earlier had industrial lock-outs and black-outs; we now have corporate burn-outs and public shoot-outs.*

That we live in an intolerant society is proved when a police constable shoots his boss because he doesn't grant him leave. A professor is stabbed by a student because he wasn't given good grades. A youngster shoots a barmaid because he is refused his drink after the bar is closed. Another schoolboy shoots at his classmates because one of them teased his girlfriend. Atrocious. And last, but not the least, at the end of the gruesome behaviour, there is no remorse – no remorse at all! The person who committed the crime, as well as the people who watched it being committed, have been rendered insensitive.

I would like to share a personal experience with you.

It was a sad day when we lost a close relative. In the afternoon we were all at the cremation ground. The man had died young, which added to the grief. As the last rites were being performed by the *Pandit,* the ladies and children wailed and cried, which moved people to tears, I overheard a conversation between two people standing behind me, that went like this:

'Did you get your visa or not?'

'No, I have yet to apply for it' came the answer. 'The US embassy has become very strict after the 9/11 attack and you better hurry', said the advisor, 'Because you have to be there to sign the agreement and we

have already invested big money.' 'Yes I know that', was the reply.

The pyre was lit by this time and one could feel the heat and smoke. They were still speaking in hushed tones, 'Are you coming for the party in the evening? It is going to be the chance of a lifetime because we will have clients from Australia as well as Europe, I feel that is a booming market now.'

The father of the man who had died broke down and people came close to him to provide moral support.

'Better be there by eight because there will be enough to catch up on, while we have a drink.'

I moved up closer to the father who was still crying. Obviously, I was neither interested nor keen to listen to the conversation any more.

If this is the progress that we have made – I wish we had not, I thought. We have become *inhuman* in the truest sense of the term.

'I like pigs. Dogs look up to us, cats look down on us. Pigs treat us as equals.'

– Winston Churchill

Violence and misery are so evidently visible around us in some form or the other, that we have become immune to all this, as if we have shut off our emotional radars. We stand firmly on the crossroads where the fog is so thick that the visibility is almost zero.

'Is it progress if a cannibal uses a knife and fork?'

– Stainis Law J. Lee

Why is This Happening to Us?

We seem to have forgotten the very basic strengths of human values and our social wealth has declined over the last 40 to 50 years because of several reasons. Our materialistic gains have, in a way, distorted the way we look at things and the way in which we attach a value to everything – a perverted perception of the value system. People, therefore, have started believing in consumerism, individualism and hedonism, that have eroded the value system and the social fabric. Social wealth, which encompasses the family, the workplace and our social circle has taken a beating on all three fronts. In a larger sense, it is an attitudinal change, which has brought in a new code of morality.

Consumerism is one of the major components of our present-day morality or value system. Control, domination and seduction of others through the possession of materialistic goods and also linking it to respect, prestige and status has given a boost to the rat race. The motto is – 'grab it, whatever it is, whatever the cost, morals be damned.' Therefore, everybody is running fast but where is everyone running to? People are climbing ladders, but often the wrong ones. Branding and marketing campaigns are adding fuel to the fire and have generated the myth that an individual will be gratified and gain an identity, only by consuming commodities. While consumerism offers the tangible good of owning a product, it does not fulfil other cultural and social requirements.

I, me and myself, i.e. *individualism* is the most important contemporary value. It propagates, promotes and makes

one believe that it frees you from the weight of family and societal constraints, that are a subtle form of slavery. So it says, 'Seek your own bliss, assert your personal rights, protect your privacy, love only yourself, do it if it feels good, be self-sufficient, fight for your personal comfort and rights, and let others be damned.' It makes you believe that you can find happiness and accomplishment without your family, without your community and without your colleagues. It says, 'You can go it alone.' This trend is breaking down families and we are heading towards a cellular, atomistic society.

Hedonism is yet another important factor of the new morality which propagates the idea that accomplishment, happiness and satisfaction are to be found in pleasure, where unrestricted sexuality is fast becoming a righteous conduct, not a shameful one. Possessing and consuming goods can also give you this pleasure and guarantee happiness. This new value system has played havoc with us and somewhere down the line, we have forgotten our traditional virtues like honour, integrity, empathy, duty, keeping commitments, trust, responsibility and even self-esteem and self-respect, that lead to cooperation in groups, families and society.

Not very long ago, families used to sit and dine together every night and weddings were a prolonged affair (in India they still are) where bonds were rejuvenated. Picnics were simple, collective outings and spending summer holidays with grandparents was a ritual, which was inspiring and satisfying. Today, we are an individualistic society with each one having his own car, his own TV, his own

freedom and his own value system. *We have accumulated a lot in the last 50 years but have forgotten what we learnt in the last 5,000 years.*

Although in the last 50 years, our value system and morality have degenerated, we still find some honest policemen, committed politicians, upright bureaucrats, loyal workers, conscientious teachers, some great corporate leaders and many down-to-earth, simple and honest citizens. Had it not been so, we would have probably by now, collapsed as a society. Unfortunately, the number of such policemen and politicians, i.e. good people in general, is fast dwindling. This trend, I feel, needs to be reversed which in itself, is a challenge.

A number of recent studies, especially those undertaken in the last two decades, point out that great corporate leadership also rests firmly on our traditional virtues and time-tested values like honesty, integrity, empathy, commitment, fair play and collective upliftment. Specifically, leaders and managers who are 'considerate' and are able to establish mutual trust, warmth and respect with the members of their group, are more effective and successful. In psychological parlance, these are the non-cognitive aspects of human abilities, whereas cognitive aspects focus on memory, intellect and problem-solving capability. By the early nineties, a lot of research had been done on the role of these non-cognitive factors in helping people succeed in both life as well as the workplace and had laid the foundation for 'Emotional Intelligence' as a concept. People with these qualities are the real winners at home, in society and at one's workplace.

These are the winners all the way.

In a broader sense, Emotional Intelligence as a hypothesis and as a model, could help people succeed in all walks of life, create great leadership, restore our value systems and rejuvenate our society.

EMOTIONAL INTELLIGENCE REDEFINED

Man has always striven to perform better, seek solace and lead a good quality of life ever since recorded history. While Gautam Buddha spoke of an equanimous mind through *Vipasana*, as early as around 600 BC, Aristotle was talking about anger management in 300 BC, but on different parts of the planet. **Great, but simple philosophies to live well as good human beings emerged 2,000 to 3,000 years ago in places like China, Arabia, India and Europe.** These taught simple, workable methods that have their basis in strong human values. Even today, we are grappling with the same problems of impulse control and managing our moods, and understanding and caring for others – in order to live a better life.

If honesty and integrity were important 500 years ago, they are important even today. If caring genuinely for your people was important in the last millennium, it would be equally important in the new millennium as well. These simple things are important universally in the corporate world, at home, on the social circuit or while leading the destinies of nations.

Albert Einstein used to teach Physics and one of his research assistants noticed that he asked one question in the final paper year after year. He went up to the Nobel Laureate and said, 'Sir, since you ask the same question every year, don't you think it is very easy for students to answer this question?' Einstein replied, 'My friend, the question remains the same, but the answer changes every year!' Theories in science and technology keep changing and every year, new methods are found to solve problems. New inventions and discoveries are made, that often challenge the old ones. That is why, the question or the problem remains the same, but the answer changes every year.

'There are many paths to the top of the mountain, but the view is always the same.'

— Chinese proverb

I feel, that in the case of human behaviour and our day-to-day living, the reverse is true. Questions and problems change year after year, but the answer remains the same – 'get back to your basics.' Our parents faced a different set of problems during their lifetime than what we faced. Our kids in turn, would face an altogether different environment during their childhood and lifetime.

In these times of constant change and turbulence, what will see us through, is the strong anchor of human values – that at the basic level, would always remain the same. An insult will remain an insult in every age and an appreciation will remain an appreciation for all days to come – its that simple.

Studies now show that leaders who won freedom for nations, leaders who were industry czars or corporate

honchos, had one common thread running through them – the basic human instinct, i.e. they were strong on human values. Especially in the corporate zone, it was not business acumen that made great leaders of them, nor was it the technical domain knowledge or financial jugglery that made the difference. What made these great leaders and high-end achievers stand apart from others – head above shoulders – were simple things like caring for their people, loving their jobs, their passion for whatever they did, high moral standards, courage of conviction, bouncing back after a setback and even just getting along well with people. In other words, they could deal with and handle their environment better than others. They were emotionally intelligent and more mature. What I have described above are the precincts of Emotional Intelligence.

Emotional Intelligence is that ability of the human race which encompasses all these basic principles, moral values and strengths of human character and willpower, that go into the making of the human temperament and personality.

In today's knowledge-cum-service based society, where human abilities to deal with our fellow beings and the environment are becoming extremely critical for survival and success, Emotional Intelligence – as an ability – becomes a forerunner of sorts. It was important, it is very important and it will be extremely important in the days to come.

Emotional Intelligence, therefore, is not a new management fad with a typical life cycle of five to six years. It is with us and will remain so – as long as we exist as 'human beings!'

'A proverb is a short sentence based on long experience.'

– Miguel De Cervantes

Emotional Roller-Coaster

The heart and the head are two machines that work non-stop –24 hours a day for us. While the heart pumps thunderously, the head ticks silently all the time, infact each supporting the other, helping us drive through our lives. Our external environment constantly gives us inputs and we react accordingly. Often, when the head rules, the heart pumps faster and when the heart feels, the head could go into a state of ecstasy, happiness or bliss. In other words, the environment around us dictates the state of our mind – often changing by the minute.

Imagine a person attending an interesting seminar, who gets a call informing him about the loss of a couple of lakhs on the share market, due to arrest of the CEO of the company on charges of financial bungling. His happiness is shattered in a minute. Yet another participant at the same seminar, gets the news of his hitting the jackpot for a lottery ticket he bought a week ago. This sends him into an all-time high. *'We own the emotions we feel, we create them by how we interpret the world.'*

What I am trying to get to, is that each one of us is on the emotional roller-coaster of life – with its own highs and lows. When the cart is going up, you shriek and you are thrilled, but when it rushes down, your heart sinks. Handling each moment of life appropriately – whenever you are on the roller-coaster – is Emotional Intelligence in the larger context. The roller-coaster takes you through dark tunnels, skirting around a mountain slope, twisting and turning, going through a loop, splashing through water at great speed; in a moment you are piercing the sky and yet, the next moment, you see the ground rushing up towards you and your heart sinks.

The art of handling ourselves *well* on this roller-coaster – which is life – is Emotional Intelligence.

Mutual Emotional Support

We need to strengthen ourselves, find innovative methods to handle the emotional turbulence, which we experience during our lifetime. We also need to provide mutual support to each other emotionally. Finding emotional support during bad times is a great help – much more than monetary or materialistic help.

> *'If you pick up a starving dog and make him prosperous, he will not bite you. This is the principle difference between a dog and a man.'*
>
> – Mark Twain

People who live in old age homes have all the comforts, medicines, food, doctors and nurses – what they don't have is someone of their own – they don't have that emotional support. They long to meet their own kids and the maximum number of deaths are during thanksgiving or during certain religious celebrations, when they want their near and dear ones to be close to them – just hold their hand or sit next to them.

Remember, even when dealing with friends and colleagues,

emotional support becomes a very important part of a long-term bondage and relationship with people.

Human Abilities, Emotional Intelligence, IQ and Success

To be able to look at the watch and tell the time is the most insignificant of human abilities. Even if no figures are written on the dials of most wrist watches today, a 10-year-old child can look at the watch and tell you the right time in less than a second. If the same input is given to a computer via a camera, it would take a large number of internal functions and interactions for the computer to be able to tell you the time!

In a quiz competition, a blurred picture of a person is shown to the participants for them to identify who the person is. One of the teams presses the buzzer and shouts – Elvis Presley!

How the human mind can handle diverse functions, adapt so quickly and learn a plethora of skills is very intriguing. The human mind works on heuristic methods (rules of the thumb or empirical rules) while computers broadly work on the algorithmic approach, which is a step-by-step, logical approach to solving a given problem.

While trying to clone human intelligence in the form of artificial intelligence, with the help of robotics and expert systems using computers, the most difficult thing for the scientific community was to define human intelligence itself.

There are so many different facets and attributes of human

abilities that it is difficult to define human intelligence in words. This is why, artificial intelligence could at best make domain-specific expert systems like medicine, oil exploration, etc. These were decision support systems and not decision-making systems that could put only 'skill-oriented' intelligence into robots. These are all, far inferior to the human brain. One practical and simplistic definition of human intelligence is given by David Wechsler as, 'The aggregate or global capacity of the individual to act purposefully, to think rationally and to deal effectively with his environment.'

This is a very generalised definition and hence cannot be used by scientists and engineers working on artificial intelligence, but it definitely points out one very important aspect of acting purposefully to deal with the environment. Here, it indicates that the 'external' (environment) becomes very important.

What I have tried to explain, is that human abilities are far too complex to be compared, captured or 'canned' in a computer. Our minds are, therefore, much more powerful than computers.

In our attempt to measure human abilities, the concept of IQ or Intelligence Quotient was developed in France in 1905.

The focus those days was on science, maths and engineering – because these were the pillars of our development. Those were the days of inventions and discoveries. Those were the days of the Wright Brothers, steam engines and electric bulbs. Obviously, therefore, tests of human abilities based on IQ also started looking towards logical reasoning, mathematical abilities, quantitative analysis, etc. These abilities were to some extent akin to the abilities of computers – that are inferior to human capabilities.

Even the best business schools till date, have written competitive tests on these lines!

Since this was the only benchmark to measure human intelligence, it became a *de facto* standard, used worldwide. Therefore, more than a million Americans were bracketed during the First World War, using the IQ method (for selection in the armed forces). IQ is believed to be God's gift and can be equated to a 'genetic lottery.'

Whatever you get, it is for keeps – you cannot ask for more. In other words, you cannot improve upon your 'gifted' IQ. It is also believed that IQ develops only up to one's teens and there is no change thereafter.

Other gifts of God like singing, painting, composing music, playing world-class cricket, writing poetry or books are somehow not accounted for by our IQ. These abilities have made celebrities out of AR Rehman, MF Hussain, Amitabh Bachchan, Javed Akhtar and Sachin Tendulkar, to name a few. The list would be fairly long. These gifts of God in terms of human abilities, have created stars in those respective fields, making them successful, rich and famous.

'Worldly human abilities', take a much simpler form, but are more difficult to define and measure. For example, how you handle your subordinate in a crisis has nothing to do with your being a mathematic buff or being a great artist who can create beautiful oil paintings. Qualities like caring for others, fighting back after a setback, managing your impulse and controlling your anger are needed by scientists and ordinary people alike. Engineers, actors, music composers, pilots, doctors, lawyers and even a joker in a circus needs these qualities.

These are the worldly human abilities, that make great national leaders, freedom fighters, successful entrepreneurs and corporate leaders. These are also the same abilities that make great fathers, teachers, mothers and above all, great friends. These abilities make strong, dependable and trustworthy human beings for you to look up to – when there is nowhere to look. They become the beacons and anchors of life when there is a storm or a typhoon. These abilities – the major areas of our discussion – put together, are the Human Emotional Intelligence.

I have briefly and broadly categorised human abilities under three heads. First, the abilities of the rational mind as defined and measured by IQ. Second, the abilities related to creativity that are truly the gifts of the gods, to a chosen few. Thirdly, the worldly abilities of mastering your own attitudes, temperament and personality, and understanding others' attitudes, represented by Emotional Intelligence.

The first two, fortunately for some and unfortunately for others, fall under the category of 'genetic bonanza.' You can do very little to improve upon them. For example, without the gift of requisite talent, a person cannot become a Pablo Picasso, a Mozart or Kishore Kumar. Similarly, without a resonable IQ level, one cannot expect to achieve much in areas that require a high IQ.

The third ability – covered under the domain of Emotional Intelligence – which makes a person excel in any of the fields is the ability to learn. There is, therefore, hope for everyone to improve upon this ability – regardless of whatever domain they may be operating in.

MULTIPLE INTELLIGENCE THEORY

The theory of multiple intelligence as proposed by Howard Gardner, talks of seven intelligences, that would broadly match up with the three domains or human abilities I have defined earlier, Briefly, these are as under:

- **Logical Mathematical Intelligence**

This is the ability to handle numbers and logical reasoning. This is the intellectual power of deduction and observation, and can be called the scientific prowess or the scientific bent of mind.

- **Linguistic Intelligence**

This is the ability to write well and handle a language to perfection. Writers, authors and poets have this.

The above two, put together, are the basis of IQ tests and also cover the domain represented by Intelligence Quotient.

- **Bodily Kinesthetic Intelligence**

This is the ability to play games and handle physical things better than others. A sportsman, as we all know, can pick up any sport very easily. He may excel only at one or two sports, but he can manage the rest very well too.

- **Musical Intelligence**

This is the ability to handle music, rhythm and beat. Again, musicians can try their hand at new instruments and learn easily because, as they say, they have music in their blood.

- **Spatial Intelligence**

This is the ability of a navigator. To find a way out of a maze and to recognise objects from different angles.

The above three put together, account for God's gift found in singers, musicians and sportsmen.

- **Interpersonal Intelligence**

People who are strong on interpersonal intelligence, have the ability to emotionally attune themselves with the needs of others. They have that subtle capability of understanding what they want. They, in general, can handle people well.

- **Intrapersonal Intelligence**

People strong on this, are capable of knowing their own feelings and emotions. They have a clear model of themselves, This is a very private kind of intelligence. People with this intelligence can guide their own behaviour very well. The above two, when put together, form the basis of Emotional Intelligence, which is the worldly ability to handle yourself and to handle others.

Research shows that 20 per cent of human abilities belong to the IQ domain, and the rest 80 per cent are other abilities like EI, creativity and artistic skills, of which a large chunk is measured by the Emotional Quotient.

Furthermore, 20 per cent success depends on IQ and 80 per cent on Emotional Intelligence and related abilities. There are examples of people with an IQ of 160, who have been failures and yet, people with an IQ below 90 have been very successful. Alternately, people with an IQ above 150, have been employed by, and work under guys with IQs less than 90. Therefore, a high IQ doesn't guarantee success.

A high IQ Engineer can be a failure as an entrepreneur or as the CEO of a company because other abilities of his, like handling people, situations or his own temper are poor. Very good film actors could jeopardise their careers if they foul-mouth their co-stars, directors or producers. Celebrities often bomb because they can't handle the press!

Emotional Intelligence, therefore, is about simple common sense, basic human values, a strong character, which actually matters for success – and is often the deciding factor between success and failure.

EI is actually about putting sense into common sense. Common sense in fact, is very common, but it is seldom used – and rarely developed. It is, therefore, required by all the people, all the time.

WHO'S EI IS IT ANYWAY?

We all have to deal with our environment, with people, with situations and above all, deal with ourselves, from one moment to another – throughout our lives. These 'essentials of life' are to be handled regardless of our caste, creed, culture, profession or gender. Emotional Intelligence deals with those inner strengths, that help us handle these essentials of life, and therefore, needs to be developed by each one of us. As I have mentioned earlier, these are learnable abilities and with conscious effort, we can handle life better.

Emotional Intelligence is like getting back to the basics, which instils those values that make us a good person, a good citizen and a good professional – in that order. This is one tool that can be effectively used in today's environment to improve upon our quality of life, create better people, managers and leaders, who are more satisfied, more caring and self-motivated. **For handling day-to-day living and dealing with our environment, Emotional Intelligence is like a Swiss knife.**

Emotional Intelligence is at play all the time. It is at play while you are deeply involved in conversation in a party, dealing with children at home, answering a phone call, handling an incident while walking down the lane or at work taking a major decision after a detailed discussion in the boardroom. Since it deals with the basic values and traits that determine our behaviour and reactions almost all the time, EI needs to be mastered by each one of us – one could be the CEO of a company, a professor, a student, a housewife or a man selling soap on the street. It is, therefore, omnipresent and omnipotent.

'If history repeats itself, and the unexpected always happens, how incapable must men be of learning from experience.'

– George Bernard Shaw

Things don't come easy. When you see Arnold Schwarzenegger with flat abdominal muscles and a great body, you must remember that he pumps iron regularly and keeps a check on what he eats. He is physically fit. Similarly, in order to keep ourselves 'emotionally fit,' we need to make a constant effort and look at our strengths and weaknesses. Improve upon your strengths further and work on your weaknesses. **Fortunately, we are 80 per cent emotionally fine.** Only 10 per cent – 20 per cent areas need to be improved upon. For example, some of us are very good at making friends, and getting along with people, but have a problem with our tempers. Such people need to work on their temper. Many have no serious problems with their temper, but call themselves 'self-centred', which means they lack empathy and they don't care much for others. They've got to look into this area.

Athletes and body builders work on their own weaknesses. Some need to develop their biceps, their shoulder muscles and some need to work on their abdomens. At the same time, they maintain their rest of their strengths – never neglecting the rest of the body. In the same way, we need to handle our emotional strengths and weaknesses in a holistic way.

Each one of us, in fact, has to move towards 'Emotional Optimisation,' which would optimise our performance in every field and bring success.

EMOTIONS AND MOTIVATION

During a parent's meet, a boy performs better on the stage, when he sees his parents sitting in the audience. It is also true that a stage actor delivers a better performance in front of the audience, than during the rehearsals, when there is no audience! His performance improves as a result of the response of the audience, or the sheer presence of people.

When you appreciate a person, he performs well because he 'feels good' and becomes motivated. When you cheer a football team from the spectators' stand, the players get charged and the team wins. When you insult a person in public, he loses heart and performs poorly thereafter. Battle cries invoke an emotional surge, which can motivate people to fight in an impossible situation and lay down their lives. There is, therefore, a strong link between the motivational and emotional state, and there is a definite link between motivation and success.

The success and failure of a person depends on his level of motivation. On a larger plain, it decides the fate of an organisation. It is estimated that in the US alone, demotivation factors cost $ 170 billion each year from low productivity. With credible governments coming in, the moods of nations change. When Rajiv Gandhi's government was sworn in during 1985, there was an upbeat mood and the stock market boomed – there was a general sense of euphoria, as if India was on the move. These were the same people, the same industry, the same resources, the same India – but the mood was different. Motivation, I feel, is a state of mind, which has to be backed by 'Emotional Arousal' and should not be seen in isolation from everything else.

What Motivates You?

Broadly speaking, there are two types of motivation. External motivation and internal/inner motivation. It is widely accepted what external motivation lasts as long as the external motivating factor does. The moment that external motivating factor disappears, motivation disappears too.

There was once a retired school teacher, an old and frail man, who lived in a house, which had a garden. Some school boys used to throw stones at his house just to tease him – they got cheap thrills out of this. All his methods to dissuade the boys from throwing stones at his house failed. He thought of a unique idea. He told the boys that he wanted to make a rockery in his garden and that he would pay them one rupee for throwing one stone – but he wanted them to select and throw only 'round pebbles' that would look good in the rockery, which he was planning to make. The boys were thrilled and started throwing in round pebbles. After 15 days, the school teacher told them that it was getting expensive and that now he would pay them only 50 paisa per stone.

Boys protested, but nevertheless, continued to throw in the stones, reluctantly. After another 15 days, the old man told them that he could pay only 5 paisa per stone.

The boys stopped throwing stones thereafter!

The analysis is as follows: initially, the boys were throwing stones just for the fun of it (inner motivation). It later got linked with payment (external motivation). The moment that the external motivation factor was withdrawn, their motivation disappeared. The first moral of the story is that you get internally motivated by simple thrills and second one is that external motivation lasts as long as the motivation factor lasts.

A boy who loves to play football, plays football even if the temperature crosses 40°C. He plays football, whether it rains or shines. He plays because he loves the game. Such motivated youngsters end up as Beckhams and Peles – star footballers. Therefore, internal motivation – that gets triggered by emotional arousal or simply on account of doing things that you want to do – is the super block on which motivation can be built to last.

The bottom line is that, as individuals, we need to find those things which give us satisfaction and that we enjoy. As managers, leaders and mentors, we must provide an 'emotionally conducive' atmosphere where people feel free to bring creativity, thrill and excitement to work. The working environment must encourage people to give their best. Today, companies are investing in swanky office spaces, cafeterias and expensive gyms to make the workplace comfortable. **What is more important, is to generate that sense of belonging, pride in the organisation, pride in doing what you are doing, camaraderie and above all, that 'feel good' factor that comes about by bringing in emotional harmony.**

PEOPLE, MANAGERS, LEADERS AND MENTORS

Managers are people who manage people. Leaders are managers with an honest heart and mentors are leaders with an honestly caring heart. Ordinary people must climb this 'emotional ladder', to become true leaders and mentors.

> *'Every Man has three characters – that which he exhibits, that which he has, and that which he thinks he has.'*
>
> – Alphonse Karr (1808–90)

Great leaders always have an emotional connect and an emotional appeal – it could be as subtle as the sex appeal. They show that they care without saying so. They hold your hand in a crisis, without blowing their trumpets about it. They show grace when you go wrong. They lead from the front without caring for themselves. You could look up to them during a catastrophe. In short, they are well-meaning and always with you.

Mentors need not always be big business leaders. You could find a mentor in your school teacher, a friend, your mother or even in your grandfather.

If you look up the Random House Dictionary, it describes the word 'mentor,' in three words, 'Trusted, Wise, Counsellor.' Leaders and managers are often wise and more often than not, they act as counsellors – they are unfortunately, not trusted often. The trust factor, I feel, is the most important one for anyone to be accepted as a leader and a mentor. People should feel comfortable with you and trust you to the hilt. Those who are led, often have great faith in the leader. Mentors have that ability to convince people about their policies, their preferences, their beliefs and their virtues. Mentors develop the skill to take people into their fold, often coaching, grooming, pushing, prodding but never shoving – like a father teaches his son how to play cricket. The greatest and the most inescapable quality in a mentor, is to provide that 'emotional crutch' or even a shoulder to cry on – if and when required.

These are the roles that we all have to play at some time or the other in our lives. As parents, as friends, as uncles and aunts, as teachers, managers and leaders – wearing different hats at different times – we must play the role of a mentor. Wherever you stand, stand tall, so that people will always look up to you.

To make a mark in life and on others, you could wear the hat of a mentor – provided you made an effort to climb this emotional ladder.

As a parting shot, I would like to say that in order to climb any ladder, it has to be you who has to make an effort – nobody can climb that ladder for you.

IN A NUTSHELL

We have made tremendous progress on the materialistic front, but unfortunately in the last 50 years, we have deteriorated badly on the humane front.

Time-tested methods and human values have been forgotten conveniently and *that* is the reason for the lack of basic consideration for each other as human beings.

We have to get back to our basics, the basics as discovered as early as the times of Gautam Buddha, Aristotle or Confucius. New scientific studies that have been undertaken to analyse the huge amount of data across various segments of professions and people, also point out that we need to look at the skills of handling people on the emotional plane. People who can connect with their teams, care for them and manage their own emotions better than others, are more successful, when compared to brilliant engineers and professionals who lack these qualities. These abilities are now called 'Emotional Intelligence' and people have got to take note of these and take action to build these abilities in individuals as well as organisations.

Emotions play an important role in our existence and we experience emotions on minute-to-minute basis – as if riding an emotional roller-coaster. Handling emotions, while on this ride – which is life – is the essence of emotional intelligence. We all need to do this. We all need emotional sensitivity – regardless of the job that we do, regardless of the span of control we have, or the levels at which we operate.

Motivation is directly linked with emotions and one cannot be expected to be motivated without emotional arousal. A large part of it has to be done by each of us individually. You have got to motivate yourself and bring about a change in your behaviour and temperament – people can only guide and persuade you, but they cannot do more than this.

In order to become leaders and mentors, we need to rise above the levels of the thinking process of mere mortals. These roles are very demanding, very challenging and require consistent, conscious efforts for one to be able to reach them. With diligent efforts, it is possible to a great extent, to achieve these. **These are the new frontiers of success.**

> 'We can easily forgive a child who is afraid of the dark; the real tragedy of life is when men are afraid of the light.'
>
> – Plato

Your Personal Road Map

1. Who is your role model? What are the five major qualities that you admire in your role model?

2. What are the qualities you feel you have that people would admire in you and look up to? List them.

3. Keeping the multiple intelligence theory in mind, list all the kinds of intelligences that you possess.

4. Be aware of the above said strengths and always remind yourself to leverage these to your advantage on a day-to-day basis.

5. List those qualities that you have, that qualify you as a mentor/leader. Now, use these qualities to guide people at home, as well at the workplace.

6. Write down any incident, where you think you have provided emotional support to someone.

7. List the human qualities that matter at
   - Home
   - Work
   - Your social circle.

8. Think of one incident, that had a deep impact on you and brought about a significant change in your life.

9. Think of one incident, where you feel you acted in a particular way in which you should not have acted and that you are still guilty about.

10. In today's hectic life, what actions do you think you can take, or you are actually taking to keep a balance between work and your life at home?

2

Human Competence:

The Length and Breadth of it all

'Not everything that can be counted counts, and not everything that counts can be counted.'

– Albert Einstein

PUTTING THINGS IN THE RIGHT PERSPECTIVE

In the last chapter, we discussed the diversity of human abilities. Such is our potential, that no single definition can possibly define human intelligence or broadly speaking – human competence. The seven intelligences, earlier described briefly, by and large, cover the entire human potential.

To recapitulate, *Scientific Competence* comprises logical, mathematical and linguistic intelligences, whereas bodily kinesthetic, musical and spatial intelligences, cover the *gifted competence* found in sportspersons, artists and musicians.

The other two – interpersonal and intrapersonal intelligences – are not as 'visible' as the scientific and gifted competencies, but are most important for our success by their presence and most contributing to our failure due to their absence! These two intelligences put together, operate in the emotional domain and can be called *Emotional Competence* or Emotional Intelligence.

These are our competency domains, that differentiate between one and the other, that also differentiate between successful people and failures amongst us. These are distinct competencies, but we always use them in a 'mix-and-match' mode. It is this interplay of basic abilities – and that too in the right proportion – which spells the difference between performers and the non-performers.

A person playing the drums and percussion instruments, needs to have his Musical Intelligence in place (music in the blood) for the rhythm and the beat, but in order to be famous and successful, he must also be able to understand and sense what the audience likes. He must also possess the physical attributes provided by the Bodily Kinesthetic Intelligence to move all four limbs with ease and grace.

A politician should be able to read the mood of the masses through emotional competence but should also be able to deliver a good speech with the help of linguistic capabilities. He also requires a bit of logic to deal with situations.

In fact, mixing emotional competence with scientific as well as gifted competence in the right proportion can produce a powerful concoction – a high octane fuel. It can be so powerful that the 'total can be greater than the sum of the parts!'

Emotional competence also gives one the will to do things. It, therefore, plays a large 'supportive role', without which other competencies collapse or their advantages are nullified. Going purely by arithmetics, Emotional Competence or Emotional Intelligence comprises two out of the seven intelligences that we have considered. This comes to less than 30 per cent of the entire human capability. But the fact of the matter is that this alone, makes a major difference between success and failure. In most cases, Emotional Competence becomes more 'augmentative' than supportive, adding that 'sheen' to performances in any domain.

After all, you require only a tablespoon of curd as a 'culture' to make lovely curd out of a kilo of milk. **Emotional Competence does to us, what a tablespoon of curd does to milk.**

A good batsman is no good, if he has no team spirit. Hitting a ball and getting it across to the boundary is not all that is expected from him. He is no good, if he has no sportsman spirit which means, taking defeat gracefully. You have to also assess the circumstances under which a batsman scores a century. With only a few wickets in hand, and a few balls to go, a batsman scores 100 runs; this shows his tenacity and ability to be able to play under pressure. There are, therefore, many supportive factors, that make a good player.

Remember, Michelangelo endured seven long years of lying on his back on a scaffold to finish his greatest piece of art – the painting on the roof of the Sistine Chapel. A good artist also needs to have resilience, perseverance and the patience to perform.

There is enough research to back up common sense – research to back up what has been true and time-tested for centuries – that emotions have been at the forefront of leadership and victory. Emotional Intelligence by itself is a grassroot-level human competence for leadership, survival and success. Emotions, I feel, were stronger in the earlier days when people cared for one another, trusted and respected others. As we traverse the path of materialistic success, we become emotionally dry – and that is a cause for concern.

THE EMOTIONAL COMPETENCE

I have now, given you a bird's eye view of what you and I are capable of, and the importance of Emotional Intelligence in the context of our 'overall abilities.' I would now, like to describe Emotional Intelligence a little more in detail.

John Mayer and Peter Salovey coined the term Emotional Intelligence sometime in the 1990s and described it as a form of 'Social Intelligence' that involves the ability to monitor one's own and others' feelings and emotions, and use this information to guide one's own thinking and action.

Daniel Goleman, around the same time, described Emotional Intelligence – breaking it down to specific competencies, that he called the framework of Emotional Competencies. Taking a closer look at these competencies will give us a better perspective of the overall Emotional Acumen which one must possess, to do well in life.

Emotional Intelligence, consisting of 20 competencies as given by Goleman is divided into four logical domains of self-awareness, self-management, social awareness and relationship management. Briefly, they are explained as under:

Self-awareness

This has three competencies:

- **Emotional Self-awareness**

This is the ability of recognising one's own feelings and how they affect one's performance. This is the starting point of self-control.

- **Accurate self-assessment**

'A true friend stabs you in the front.'

– Oscar Wilde

This is the ability to know your own strengths and weaknesses. People, high on this component, are aware of their abilities and limitations. They are prepared to learn from others, take candid feedback and learn from their mistakes. This, I feel, is one of the most important of human abilities, because this is the starting point for any positive change to occur. One can see that new actors who make their screen debut, improve after a few movies. These are the guys who have no inhibitions and are prepared to learn from their senior artists, co-artists and directors. Then, there are some who refuse to learn because they 'feel' they are the best. These guys never make it big and they fade out in no time.

Remember, if you want to improve your game of tennis, listen to the coach and play with a better player. The rest will automatically follow.

This ability is found in almost all star performers. Average performers, typically over-estimate their strengths, whereas top performers are more conservative about their own abilities. If anything, they will under-estimate their abilities. This also indicates that star performers set very high standards for themselves. This ability is highly learnable. If you are not taking feedback and reflecting on your performance from time to time – it's time that you start doing this – because it is important and very much possible to do this. But it requires some effort and courage to admit one's weaknesses, to start with.

- **Self-confidence**

People with self-confidence always come out as winners. **There is a difference between being confident and being foolhardy.** Self-assessment tells you, how much you can achieve and self-confidence tells you that yes, you can achieve whatever you have set your sights on.

Self-Management

This has six competencies.

- **Self-control**

This is the prowess that star performers possess. **The ability to remain calm and unflappable during stressful situations is a great quality that only leaders have.** Business executives, who are high on this component, can handle their teams better and provide that soothing touch to their subordinates when they need it most. This is expected from military leaders, skippers on the cricket pitch and all those who have to motivate people to accomplish organisational goals. Self-control also takes into account, managing your moods, anger and impulses.

'We boil at different degrees'

– Ralph Waldo Emerson

- **Trustworthiness**

This has a large moral component attached to it. People high on this are forthright, have clear and good intentions, are principled and demonstrate all these abilities loud and clear.

- **Conscientiousness**

Conscientious people are self-starters. They are scrupulous and responsible people who keep things going without anyone supervising them. This is a desirable trait in any job.

- **Adaptability**

In today's scenario, when 'change management' is the *mantra*, adaptability lets you handle that change and becomes a very important ability in that context. These people can handle uncertainties, are creative, open to new ideas and always ready to move on. **Opportunities are never lost, someone will take the ones that you missed.**

- **Achievement drive**

This is the key to motivation and gives one the sense to compete with oneself, striving to continually improve one's performance. This ability is also linked with hope, optimism and a positive outlook without which, one cannot handle obstacles and setbacks that come our way. These people follow the dictum, *'you never win the Silver but you always lose the Gold.'*

- **Initiative**

Self-starters, these people don't require pushing and prodding to take action. People high on this, take pre-emptive action and are pro-active rather than reactive in their approach.

Being conscientious, taking initiative and having an achievement drive are the key components of self-motivation.

Social Awareness

It consists of three competencies:

- **Empathy**

This is a person's ability to be concerned about others,

to know and feel what their needs are. Such people have a high emotional connect with people whom they deal with. These are people who can understand others very well.

- **Service orientation**

For the present-day corporate, where a large part of the business is service-based, service orientation is a very important competence. The need to understand and satisfy one's customer is the basic requirement of good customer relationship.

- **Organisational awareness**

This is the ability to read the pulse of an organisation. This ability also helps you sense the power centres of the organisation and build strong personal networks with the people who matter. In the corporate world, this is the competence of star performers.

Relationship Management

This has eight competencies:

- **Developing others**

This ability is the instinct to act as a coach. This is not only required by frontline managers, but is also needed in a higher-end leadership, where one is expected to provide mentoring and guidance.

- **Influence**

Influencing others, is the ability to manage emotions in others. Those who can influence and persuade, can lead effectively. This is the ability that is present in most star performers and effective leaders.

- **Communication**

To be able to get your point across to the other person, is a great ability. To be able to listen to others and simplify things while making a case, and being diplomatic when required, make you a good communicator.

- **Conflict Management**

Handling a situation before it snowballs, is a highly desirable trait in managers and leaders. The art of picking up signals to smell trouble as it is about to brew and calming down those involved, is a great skill. This is extremely useful, while negotiating deals or handling tough situations between groups within an organisation, like the management and the workers' union.

'It takes two flints to make a fire.'

– Louisa May Alcott

- **Leadership with a vision**

This ability lets you inspire people to work towards a common goal. It enables the leader to arouse enthusiasm for a shared objective.

- **Change catalyst**

This is the ability to usher in change smoothly, also keeping the organisation in a dynamic state by bringing in new ideas and fresh initiatives.

- **Building bonds**

Networking is the emotional ability that helps make strong bonds with people. It also builds trust and friendship.

- **Teamwork and collaboration**

No single person can achieve or should even attempt to achieve everything by himself. This is the quality of star performers. They work in teams, nurture collective efforts and collaborate to succeed. They understand the strength of teamwork and are always willing to work in a team. They are essentially team players. Whichever way we look at it, these abilities are very important in order to handle our day-to-day affairs, situations, leadership and eventually take ourselves towards success.

The Organisation's Approach to Assessing People

Organisations use certain parameters to assess their employees.

These parameters are highly company-centric and vary according to the job profile and the level of the employee.

Armed forces the world over, require a high degree of leadership and motivation, and some major parameters used by them for assessing officers are from the emotional plane.

For example, the best armies of the world, give a very high weightage to the following, while assessing their officer cadre.

- **Drive, determination and decisiveness**

Which means vigour, the will to achieve, decision-making under pressure and the determination to succeed against all odds.

- **Dependability**

This implies the intensity of involvement, trustworthiness and the ability to carry out a task without being prodded or pushed.

- **Integrity**

This is directly linked to honesty and good character at a very deep level.

- **Loyalty**

The extent to which a person can provide faithful and loyal support to his superiors and subordinates.

- **Moral courage**

The courage of conviction and intellectual honesty.

In the armed forces, the above qualities are known as star qualities. Any leader at any level is expected to score very high gradings on these. Scores on these qualities are evaluated very critically during the promotion process.

Apart from this, there are parameters like maturity, tenacity, ingenuity, initiative, dedication to the organisation, the ability to motivate the team and communication skills.

A 360-degree officer evaluation system of one of the best armies in the world reads briefly as:

- This officer is always ethical and cares more about the Army, his command and his soldiers.
- The officer leads by example.
- I'd follow this officer in combat and trust this officer leading my family members or close friends into combat.

- This officer possesses the moral and intellectual capacity to serve the nation as a commissioned officer.

All these parameters cover a major portion of the Emotional Competence framework as elucidated by Goleman. Therefore, it would be good to keep in mind that Emotional Intelligence comprises a large set of abilities that have been studied and used by a large number of organisations for many years in different contexts, sometimes with different names, for different people at different levels of the hierarchy.

'A woman is like a tea bag – only in hot water do you realize how strong she is.'

– Eleanor Roosevelt

It has also been widely accepted, after due research that both men and women, fare equally well on the emotional acumen. They may, however, have strengths and weaknesses in different skills of the emotional domain.

Therefore, Emotional Competence was always an area of interest for researchers and in a way, even in the modern context, Emotional Intelligence is not really new.

Whether new or not, the fact remains that there is now, growing awareness that these competencies are very important at the workplace as well as the home. These abilities are important to the extent that they can make all the difference between success and failure in every profession.

EMOTIONAL COMPETENCIES ARE LEARNABLE

Common sense tells us that these competencies are learnable.

Common sense also tells us that we learn these from each other, from parents, teachers, friends, bosses, peers and subordinates. Strictly speaking, there is no single teacher. And for one, we have to become our own teachers – a lot can be learnt on our own. Emotional learning is like moving towards an emotionally disciplined life and making yourself emotionally fit.

These things are learnt early in life, during our most impressionable years. We observe what our friends do, we also observe what our parents and grandparents tell us. The company we keep, the books we read, the hobbies we develop, all of these have a profound effect on our overall development, especially in the emotional domain. These are told to us during childhood and our adolescence through anecdotes and personal experiences by the people we come into contact with at home and in school. As we grow, we don't stop learning. In fact, we learn the same way as we had learnt earlier, by observing people, by emulating those whom we admire, by reading about people who did well and through their biographies. The major difference between learning during adulthood and childhood is that, as adults, we have a larger capacity to use reasoning and argument before we accept any idea, than when we were small kids.

A native American boy was talking to his grandfather. 'What do you think about the world situation?' he asked. The grandfather replied, 'I feel, two wolves are fighting in my heart. One is full of anger and hatred, and the other is full of love, forgiveness and peace.' 'Which one will win?' asked the boy, to which the grandfather replied, 'The one I feed.'

– Origin unknown.

As adults, we can take advantage of our logical reasoning to make suitable amends for our behaviour – with others and how well we behave with ourselves. At every stage of life, we meet people who influence our behaviour. We read books that make a difference to our thinking process, we see and get influenced by movies, that send a strong message. We are also influenced by incidents, newspapers, magazines and organisations that make strong appeals.

This, therefore, is an ongoing learning process. The bottom line is that it all depends on you and which way you want to go. **Don't expect to lose weight when your neighbour goes on a diet! The efforts have to be all yours.**

As you go along; these chapters will unfold many avenues for you. This can make a huge, positive difference to you, which would change things for the better at the workplace, social environment and home. **I am sure, that it will change the way you look at things, your overall perspective and the way that you deal with people and motivate your heart.**

IN A NUTSHELL

Human potential is very vast. It is neither easily definable, nor easily measurable. Broadly speaking, our competence falls under three categories, i.e. Scientific Competence, which is related to logic and maths, the Gifted Competence related to the arts and games and the Emotional Competence related to intrapersonal and interpersonal skills.

Emotional Competence plays a very dominating role by itself to ensure success or failure. It also has an augmentative effect on our other competencies, be it of a scientific or 'gifted' category.

Although corporates, governments and armed forces across the world have been using Emotional Competence as a major input to assess and evaluate personnel for a very long time now, there has been a recent realisation, say for the last 8 to 10 years, that Emotional Competence is most important for success and satisfaction. It is also important to understand that Emotional Competence or Emotional Intelligence becomes more important for people positioned at the higher end of the professional hierarchy. The learning process starts early in life, during our most impressionable years. But this process continues through one's teens and adulthood. We continue to learn through our experiences, reading books, listening to good people, working in good organisations, all the time picking up cues in order to improve our quality of work, relationships at work and home and most of all, looking for ways and means to live well – successfully and satisfactorily.

'At first people refuse to believe that a strange new thing can be done, then they begin to hope it can be done, then they see it can be done – then it is done. And all the world wonders why it was not done centuries ago.'

– Frances Hodgson Burnett

Your Personal Road Map

1. List five Emotional Competencies, that you feel, are your strengths.

2. What can you do to improve self-control?

3. From now onwards, make a conscious effort to read the pulse of your organisation for which you work, by closely observing the behaviour of the people. Use this to develop strong relations with people.

4. What do you think is your biggest strength? How do you think you can leverage it?

5. What do you think is your biggest weakness? How do you think you can work on it?

6. Keeping in mind the 20 Emotional Competencies discussed in the chapter, list five of your strong as well as weak competencies.

Strong   **Weak**

3

Powers of Positive Emotions:

The Emotional Juggernaut

'A person gets from a symbol the meaning he puts into it.'

— The United States Supreme Court

HUMAN EMOTIONS

Most of us who love animals, know of the emotional bonds that we develop with our pets at home. If you leave your dog with the neighbour when you go on a holiday, the dog stops eating because it is sad. When you come back home, it welcomes you by wagging its tail. This happens because animals, just as humans, have strong emotions. But is there any difference between human emotions and the emotions that animals have? Yes, there are broadly three major differences.

First, the range of emotions in humans is far greater than in animals. We undergo feelings of passion, compassion, exuberance, guilt and ego to name a few, that animals don't. Even if they do, they can't properly express all of these complex feelings.

Secondly, within each emotion there are fine gradations, that are present in and are expressed by humans. These fine gradations are not available to animals. When you are happy, you can grin, smile or laugh. You could just smile with your eyes – or just look happy. It often happens with all of us that we look at a friend or a family member and say, 'Oh, you look very happy today,' without that person giving specific indication of being happy. We, therefore, express our feelings strongly and have sensitive emotional antenna to pick up the minutest of emotional signals from others.

A person rang up his friend who was on a holiday on an island. He asked his friend, 'How do you pass your time on the island?' His friend said that he passed his time by playing cards with his dog. 'Who wins?' came the next obvious question. 'Me of course' was the answer. The person immediately remarked, 'But how come you are winning? Your dog is very intelligent!'

His friend said, 'Yeah, my dog is very intelligent, but whenever I deal the cards and my dog gets a good hand, he gets very excited and starts wagging his tail! I pack my hand, and that is why I am winning.'

This little joke indicates the third and the most powerful difference between human emotions and the emotional abilities of the rest of the living species, 'The power to choose to display, or not to display an emotion.' We as humans, can choose to wag or not to wag our tail when we are happy. Also, we possess the smartness to display an appropriate emotion at an appropriate time for an appropriate purpose. This single ability available to us – *but not always used* – is the most effective strength, which, if developed and used appropriately can make all the difference between success and failure; a winner and a loser.

Why Did Nature give us Emotions?

On the face of it, and as we use the word 'emotions' in our day-to-day conversation, one would simply say that emotions are meant to display our feelings – in other words, to help us express ourselves. But, if one delves a little deeper, one would realise that emotions play a very important role in our lives – so much so, that our entire life and survival depends upon them. Going back into the evolution of mankind, it is a scientifically proven fact that the emotional brain developed much earlier than the rational brain. **The emotional brain gave us the strengths and the sense to handle situations and to deal with our environment.** This was that basic instinct which helped us survive in a tough, uncertain environment where the rule of 'survival of the fittest' applied to humans, animals and birds alike. I would like to specify four major areas where emotions play an important role in our daily lives:

- In our survival.

- While handling situations.

- Making us see beyond the obvious.

- In giving us the strength to conquer failure.

There could be many other facets of emotional acumen that include expressing ourselves, our moods and behaviours. It is worthwhile to look at the four areas listed above.

Our Survival

When you see someone approach you threateningly, brandishing a knife, you don't start worrying about the length of the knife or try to find out if it is sharp on both sides. You either take out a gun (if you have one), you look around for a stick or a stone to hit back with, or you scream and scram from the scene. This is a 'shoot or scoot' (or fear) reaction that we have been endowed with, for our survival. You find the best way out under the given circumstances! Our emotional brain developed, giving us this instinct to survive the predators, jungle fires and floods during our evolution. These instincts are inherited through our genes and still help us handle dangerous situations even though, life has become much more organised in the last 200 to 400 years. These 'survival instincts' have become outdated and are not so relevant today. At the same time, when there is a trying situation, we all do react, using these ancient basic instincts – overreacting very often, with disproportionate responses that can be dangerous at times, for us and for others.

That is why, a minor argument between two people can sometimes end up in a dangerous brawl or a shootout. We need to keep these instincts in check, using our rational mind.

A programme on *Discovery Channel* or on *Animal Planet* is enough to illustrate that all animals and birds protect their offspring. They protect them, train them and let go only once that their young ones become sure-footed and can fend for themselves. Similarly, a mother's love for her child also protects the child from harm. A mother's instinctive love in fact, is so strong, that it lasts from the womb to the tomb. The smallest of animals fight back to protect their offspring – so that the species can survive. Therefore fear, the maternal instinct, our anger to hit out and 'heart over head' instincts are emotions that all of us are endowed with, for our survival.

Our parents love us so much that they go out of their way to give us the best that they can afford. They look after us throughout our childhood and even thereafter. Somewhere down the line, we as humans have gone wrong. Many children, somehow, do not look after their parents when they need them. We get so drawn in by the pulls and pressures of modern lifestyles, that we don't have any time left for those who brought us up with unconditional love. We can't blame it on nature, because nature has given us love for our parents. We will have to take the blame on ourselves, because we are running after that glitter and gold, often forgetting our basic duties and responsibilities.

Handling Situations

A woman is driving back home on a highway with her toddler, when her car skids and dangerously turns over, throwing her out but trapping the kid under it. Immediate help is not available, because the incident takes place at the dead of the night. This frail woman, all of 55 kg, in a state of panic, is left with no choice but to do something on her own. With tears flowing down her cheeks, she runs to the car that weighs 3,000 pounds and pushes it over to save her child! In doing so, she hurts her backbone seriously but manages to save the child. This is the strength that an 'emotional surge' can give us -- it makes us do things, that are normally not possible for us to do.

A soldier goes into the minefield through a barrage of bullets to bring back his injured friend. He knows he is in mortal danger, but the emotional bond gives him the courage to move and act.

Tom and Jack were childhood friends who joined the Army and were lucky enough to join the same battalion. Their unit was sent to war. In the thick of the battle, Tom was badly injured and lay in a trench, crying in pain for help. There was constant and heavy shelling outside, and Jack, with a few of his comrades, was held up in a nearby bunker. Jack wanted to run through the barrage of firing to reach the trench and help his best friend. His comrades tried to persuade him, not to take the risk. After a while, Jack decided otherwise and ran up to the trench through the heavy firing. Unfortunately, Jack returned empty-handed and announced tearfully that Tom was dead. 'Was it worth the trouble, running to the trench to get Tom?' asked his comrades. 'Yes', said Jack, 'Because when I reached the trench, Tom was alive and before he died, he said, "Jack I knew you would come".' These are the strengths, bonds and rewards of emotions − when you can expect the unexpected.

These inner strengths, very often, give us the courage to rise up to an occasion. **If such bonds and affiliations can be built and strengthened in organisations, among people, between family members and friends, we would be able to make people rise up to levels beyond materialistic thinking.** These build trust and camaraderie, that cannot be quantified. These are the relations that are built to last.

Seeing Beyond the Obvious

Nature has given us instincts that go beyond the powers of the rational mind. When everything appears to be OK at the surface, and logic give us the go-ahead, there is still a feeling lurking somewhere at the back of our minds telling us, 'I smell a rat.' This internal radar can sometimes come to our rescue and help us take decisions that are best suited for us. There is no explanation, but it does happen. This kind of intuition, hunch, gut feeling or the 'sixth sense' is experienced by many of us.

We normally work with two minds, one that thinks and analyses and the other that feels and senses. Many top corporate professionals and decision-makers say that they rely heavily on the latter, this inner voice or intuition while taking decisions.

Personalities like Gandhi, Churchill and Einstein attributed a large part of their success to intuition.

In today's environment, especially in the turbulent business environment, the parameters, variables, market forces and imponderables are so many, that one can calculate and plan up to a limit. Beyond that, one has to rely on something beyond the rational and *that* is this 'inner radar.' This radar can tell you to go for it or not to go for it – but it can't give you the basis of its calculations. These intuitions come at odd times, maybe when you are alone with yourself, when your mind is free to work on its own. But, these feelings help all of us at some point or the other in our lives.

Courage to Conquer Failure

'Success is moving from failure to failure without losing enthusiasm.'

– Winston Churchill

Heard that story in school about the spider trying to climb the wall again and again? Yes, we all have. To some extent or the other, we all have the courage to fight back after a failure. Those who have it in them, succeed in handling failure and get what they want – success. Many of us give up too soon. Nature has given us the ability to take denials and failures in our stride and yet try and patiently reach our goals. Virtues like patience, determination, will power and perseverance, help us make repeated attempts. This is emotional resilience. Thomas Edison failed 999 times before he could make an electric bulb.

Sales and marketing people who take each rejection from their clients as a challenge and get back to the next client with renewed vigour and a fresh selling strategy, achieve higher sales targets. There have been authors who were rejected by many publishers, but could at the end of the day, come out with a bestseller.

Emotional resilience, adaptability and keeping up your enthusiasm is the difference between those who succeed and who don't.

Remember – nature has given each one of us enough will power – we are the ones who forget to test and try it. God never gives us a burden that our shoulders and heart cannot bear.

A woman's husband returned after fighting a battle for his country. The scars of war brought about a big change in him and he became a social recluse, an introvert, living like a vegetable. The lady tried to bring him out of his mental trauma but failed, time and again. Her neighbours advised her to go to a monk who would find a way to cure her husband. The monk agreed to concoct a potion, but he needed a lion's whisker to make it. The lady had no option but to set forth towards the jungle to look for a lion. She located a lion's den and the next day, took some food for him. She stood at a distance from the den. A lion saw her but did not approach her because she was at a great distance. Everyday, she came with food for the beast and gradually started moving closer and closer to the den. One day, she came very close to the den and the lion came out. By this time, he was used to the lady and ate the food she had brought him. This went on for a few days and she even started petting the lion, that now, enjoyed her company. One day, the lady cleverly plucked his whisker and came home excited with her achievement. She ran straight to the monk and demanded that he prepare the potion. The monk took the whisker, lit a fire and threw in the whisker – burning it to ashes. 'What are you doing?' asked the lady, 'I spent so much time getting it. You were supposed to make a potion with this for my husband!' The monk replied, 'Lady, if you had spent so much time and shown patience with your husband, as you did while getting the lion's whisker, he would have been cured by now.'

'It takes twenty years to make an overnight success.'

– Eddie Cantor

The moral of the story is that we give up too soon. Patience and perseverance pay in the long run.

The very fact that nature has given us emotions, tell us about the important role they play in our lives. From our basic survival to handling situations, facing life, seeing beyond the obvious and fighting against all odds, is all that is required to live a rich and full life. What I have described, can be seen as the emotional fabric, which is given to us by nature. I would like to now, look at those fine 'emotional strands' that go into the making of the emotional fibre. The stronger the strands, the stronger the fibre and the better the emotional fabric. I am going to take major ones, that have the power to transform our personalities. As you go along, please see your own weaknesses in the light of each strand. Make a note to improve upon these weaknesses. Remember, you will have to do it yourself – no one else can do it for you. I can only point out the importance of these very basic human essentials. Also, don't forget to identify your strengths and be proud of them. After all, nature does perform its balancing act – you have strengths as well as weaknesses. Being proud is not good enough for you. Leverage your strengths to make your life more meaningful, taking these as personal basic building blocks to motivate yourself and move towards success.

Delayed Gratification

A generation ago – not very long back – people were proud of saving from their earnings to buy a car, a house or even a carpet for their homes. There was, in fact, always a sense of pride and a sense of achievement when you bought something after you waited for it so long. People were prepared to wait. **This single quality has in its folds, pride, the sense of achievement, patience, perseverance, discipline, a bit of sacrifice, will power and implicit in all these, what we all so boastfully talk about – self esteem. It is not what you achieved that is important, but how you achieved it.**

You would always be more attached emotionally, to something that you bought when your sweat went into buying it.

When a football team wins a match, it is the shield that matters – not the price tag on the shield! You like gifts but you would love what you bought from your own hard-earned money – what you toiled for.

In a nutshell, this is the ability of delayed gratification. The ability to impose delay on impulse – not to give in to temptation, which is an easier way out. Today, we live in a society of instant gratification, shortcuts, 'buy now, eat now, pay later' – and sometimes, never.

When we talk of delayed gratification, there is a sense of purpose and a goal to be achieved. It is like the experience that a mountaineer goes through, putting in every ounce of energy to reach the summit. This spirit lets you move towards the goal, when you know the goal is far away. This quality, in fact, reflects a strong character. **Courage is not always a bold and heroic act, it is often a quiet voice within you, which softly whispers – 'let's try again'.**

Mr Rajinder Pawar who is the Chairman of NIIT, was known to be extremely meticulous during his engineering days at IIT Delhi. His batchmates say that he would finish things at hand and only then, go to sleep. If he decided that he would finish certain chapters and write a letter to his father before going to bed – rest assured, he would do it. Friends from his college days attribute his success majorly to this strong trait, which he demonstrates till date.

These are the people who have that sense of pride, that sense of achievement and a dogged perseverance. They grow up to be self-righteous and do not take short-cuts, don't break queues, wait for their turn and take only what is actually their due. These are the people who deny bribes and are always grateful to those who ever helped them, anytime in their lives. These are the mountain goats who would push hard and climb mountains.

Kids who at very young age, demonstrated the ability to control their impulses, showed signs of will power and character. These kids grew up to be more socially compatible, could handle setbacks, take things (failures and successes) in their stride, and were more responsible professionals. Those who demonstrated a timid attitude towards controlling their impulses were more prone to frustration, blaming others, had low self-esteem and found it difficult to control stress as they grew up and faced life. This, in fact, is a 'mega emotional ability.'

Basic things taught in schools and practiced at home, like fasting, sharing food with friends and family, making little sacrifices for a cause, the habit of saving out of a meagre earning, living within your means, standing in a queue, waiting for your turn and charity are the seeds that help develop this mega habit. Those who can develop this, are sure to be successful in life. They are good people, good citizens and good workers – an asset to society.

To be in Flow – Ecstasy in Performance

We have all appeared in various written tests and examinations. We prepare seriously for each exam. But then, there are days when we perform poorly and days when we perform brilliantly – despite the same amount of preparation. On certain days, tennis players can get each service across the net as an 'ace' – and they don't know why. This happens to golfers, cricketers and athletes too!

These are the moments of ecstasy when all our abilities and faculties get synchronised and aligned to give us that optimum performance. In other words, we are in absolute flow – like a waterfall.

This emotional state occurs between anxiety and boredom, that optimum mix. During an interview if you are too 'edgy', you can't perform because you are nervous. You will do equally badly if you are too relaxed and wouldn't be able to muster up the right stance as well as the right answers.

A star performer in any field is a star performer if he can get into flow at will. Shah Rukh Khan, in one of his TV interviews was asked the secret of his success. He said that getting up every morning for 10 years consistently, with same enthusiasm and giving a shot in front of the camera with the same ardour, exuberance and consistency was possibly the most important reason for his success.

In a state of flow, one can expect an effortless peak performance where you beat yourself to the finishing line – out-perform yourself. This can happen to people in diverse professions, like engineers, scientists, designers, surgeons, chess players and managers.

Absolute, undivided attention and concentration,

coupled with an optimum anxiety level, enthusiasm and passion would make that potion for ecstasy and bliss while a job is being performed. **People perform well when they love what they are doing.** They do it, because they have a sense of satisfaction, fun, even relaxation when they do it. In other words, their hearts are in the jobs that they love to perform. For them, it is a yearning – it beckons them and they are happy just doing it – which itself is their biggest reward. Therefore, excellence and flow can be achieved in areas that give you sheer pleasure and not in those that you are pushed into.

Meditation techniques teach relaxation and help one concentrate. *Vipassana*, for example, is a meditation technique which helps keep a calm mind. It also helps one concentrate and even improves one's ability to read faster, absorb faster and retain better. It can help one achieve peak performance, provided one enjoys performing!

Empathic Resonance – The Emotional Radar

There was once a boy, who went to a pet shop to buy a pup. The shopkeeper let loose six cute little pups for the boy to select one from. The boy noticed one pup which was limping, picked it up and said, 'I want this one. How much do I pay?' The shopkeeper told the boy that this pup would not be able to play and run as it had a defective leg by birth, and that if he wanted to, he could take it for free. The boy insisted that he wanted to take the same pup and was prepared to pay the $5 displayed on the window, for the pups. Once the deal was closed and the boy was about to leave with the lame pup, the shopkeeper asked the boy why he had insisted upon buying the lame pup. The boy quickly rolled up his trousers and showed the shopkeeper that he was wearing an artificial leg. He said, 'I will be able to understand how he feels because I too, cannot run as fast as all my other friends.'

The moral of the story is: put yourself in others' shoes. Do to others, what you would do to yourself.

This is called empathy. When you tell someone, 'I understand how you feel', it is sympathy, but when you say, 'I feel how you feel', then it is empathy. When there is an emotional connect, there is genuine empathy. We often sympathise, but we do not often empathise with others.

Remember, at home, at work or with friends, if you don't have genuine feelings for others, you will be a disaster. Good leaders have this quality of caring for their team, whatever be the level of leadership. A football coach can guide and handle the team better, when he can connect with individual players and cares for each person and his requirements. **To handle yourself, use your head – to handle others use your heart.**

Leaders consistently make efforts to develop and enhance the ability to know how others feel. Even during the days of the industrial economy, great manufacturing companies that cared for their employees and workers made huge profits, had no lock-outs and earned the goodwill of workers and their associates.

When an employee or a team member needs help and you go out of your way to help him, he always remembers you for the good turn that you did. Remember, this goes a long way. **Helping people during personal crisis builds a very strong bond. A mishap in the family, the loss of a near and dear one, or handling a divorce are devastating experiences. These are emotional crises when a person needs emotional support.** As a leader or a friend, you are expected to provide such support. Remember, we are all a part of each other's emotional support kit and all of us, at one time or another, need an emotional crutch. **All that a person needs sometimes, is a hand to hold and a heart to understand.**

While feeling how others feel and responding to their needs is important, demonstrating your own reactions and feelings appropriately, is also very important. What you must say at the right place, at the right time and to the right person, in the right manner and in the right tone, can spell the difference between success and failure. The mode of the rational mind is words, whereas, the mode of emotions is non-verbal. *How* you say something, becomes more important than *what* you say – and *where* you say it. Imagine a board meeting where the Chairman tells a vice president, 'Is this the way to write a report? It is absolutely unacceptable!' These words can have a devastating affect on a very senior colleague, who would possibly be dumbstruck for the rest of the meeting, and may even lose his sleep for a couple of days. We often say things that we never mean! Then why speak such words? In the case of the Chairman's remark, he actually never meant it seriously, but it had serious repercussions. **'Managing your mouth', and taking care of other people's sensitivity is an extremely important aspect of our day-to-day living.**

'Never be sarcastic', is an old saying. This is another aspect of *how* you say things and not *what* you say. A pungent tongue and a caustic remark hurts, and hurts like hell. This can became a serious problem in relations at home, in one's social circle and at work. So, watch out when you say something!

As you deal with people, you come to know about their emotional responses and sensitivities. If you develop this skill, it acts like an 'emotional radar', picking up weak as well as strong emotional signals from others – always guiding you to respond appropriately.

It is not more light that is needed in the world, it is more warmth. We will not die of darkness but of cold.

Listening to others is also an important part of caring and demonstrating that you care. Remember, *demonstration* is very important for your credibility. **In many cases, listening properly or giving someone a 'patient hearing', means that half the battle is won. Once you lend an emotional ear, the person feels satisfied, confident and relaxed. This also builds trust.**

How you listen is important. Many books and seminars tell you, that in order to be a good listener, you must look into a person's eyes and nod after a few minutes to show him that you are listening, raise your eyebrows once in a while during the meeting and grunt at least once during the conversation. For God's sake, a monkey in a zoo can be taught to do all this! You could be doing all this and yet not listening! The worst is that when you behave like a monkey, and are not listening to the other guy, he knows that you are not paying attention. We all have such experiences where the person is listening to you, and yet not listening – he is seeing through you as if you do not exist.

Therefore, keep your radar tuned and make that emotional connect. Try it and you will see – it works!

Charity and the 'Do Good' Factor

While empathy is about feeling how others feel and putting yourself in others' shoes, charity and benevolence is about doing something for those who need something more than you. Charity is the attitude to help others.

There was an old lady who had lost her husband a while ago. She lived in an old age home and didn't keep good health. She used to send a cheque to the caretaker every month, who would offer flowers on her husband's grave. Her health was failing and a time came, when she felt that she might not live for very long. She decided to go to her husband's grave and offer him flowers with her own hands, maybe for the last time. She was taken by the staff of the old age home in a wheelchair to the caretaker, who accompanied her to the grave. The old lady looked happy and satisfied as she offered the flowers and prayed for her husband's departed soul. As she was sitting pretty on the wheelchair, the caretaker remarked, 'All of us spend so much time and money, offering flowers and candles to the dead, who are not even alive to appreciate these gestures. I wish we made such efforts for those who live and suffer in this world.' The lady didn't respond, and went back without saying a word. The caretaker knew that he had said something harsh which the old lady didn't appreciate. As expected, the cheques stopped coming in.

After a couple of years, as the caretaker sat in his office, there was a knock on the door and a very graceful lady entered the room. The caretaker couldn't recognise her and before he could say anything, the lady told him that she was the one who used to send him money for the flowers on her husband's grave. She said that she had taken his suggestion seriously – and thereafter started helping the poor and those who suffered and languished in homes for the aged. She started this mission from her wheelchair, but derived so much satisfaction, that it gave her the strength to get up and walk, and in few months, she found a reason to live for. She was hale and hearty now.

The moral of the story is that if you help others, it gives you tremendous satisfaction, strength, health and high self-esteem.

Charity does not mean pulling your wallet out and donating money. Charity could be about doing good in any form. If you are in a position to help someone and you do, that is charity. If you, with your experience and wisdom can guide a student to take up the right career, then too, it is charity. On a cold, wintry night, if you can cover a small, shivering pup with a blanket, it is charity. To help the community in any way is charity. Even grooming and mentoring is a form of charity. The feeling is more important than the act itself.

I was going to the airport to pick up someone in Delhi. At a traffic intersection, a poor old lady started crying for help. Her daughter was lying on the road. She informed us that she was pregnant and in pain. She wanted us to take her to the hospital for the delivery. We wanted to help her, but since we were going to the airport and couldn't afford to waste time, I gave her a bottle of water and Rs 200 so that she could take her daughter to the hospital. As I narrated this incident to my friends in the evening, I was told that it was a regular trick played on unassuming people by a gang that operated in Delhi. I felt cheated, but on second thoughts, I felt that what I had done, was a good gesture to help someone in distress. My intention was to help out and I did what any good person should have done.

Even in a society full of tricksters and cheats, let us not forget our personal emotional responses. Those 200 rupees that I gave away, were not a loss but a big gain. In my heart of hearts, I felt that I had helped someone. What matters, is the way that you look at things.

Mahatma Gandhi was once travelling by train. As he was getting into the train, one of his shoes came off and fell on the track. Since the train was moving, he could not get down to retrieve it. He quickly took off the other shoe and threw it on the track. The other passengers asked him why he did that and he said, 'The poor fellow who finds it will be able to use the shoes as now it is a pair.'

'I shall pass through this world but once. Any good thing I can do, or any kindness I can show to any human being, let me do it now and not defer it. For I shall not pass this way again.'

– Stephen Grellet

There was once a person, who was walking on the sea beach. He saw another person walking far ahead of him. He was picking up something from the ground and throwing it into the water. The man quickly moved closer to that person and noticed that he was picking up starfish that had been washed onto the beach and was throwing them back into the water. Astonished, he asked, 'why are you throwing these fish back into the water?' The man answered with a smile, 'Otherwise, they will all die lying here on the beach.' The man asked, 'But there are thousands of these fish lying on this beach, do you think it will matter?' The other person picked up a fish and throwing it back into the sea said, 'It will matter to this one.'

The moral of the story is that it does not matter *how much* you do or for *how many*, so long as you do something for someone who needs it. And *that* is what matters.

'A pessimist is the one who, when he has the choice between two evils, chooses both.'

– Oscar Wilde

Hope and Optimism

If you read biographies and autobiographies of the rich and the famous, the high and the mighty, the movers and shakers – most of them were optimists throughout their formative days. They struggled and grappled with circumstances – but with a positive outlook, hope and optimism. You pick up anyone whom you consider to be successful, a company president, a successful industrialist, a great film actor, a music director or an Olympic gold medalist. They all had one thing in common – they were persistent and had strong hopes of ultimately doing well.

Hope and optimism are country cousins. It means believing, that you have both the will and the way to accomplish your goals, whatever these may be. It is that positive attitude towards life and achievement, which makes people successful. Hope brings enthusiasm into working towards your goals. The ability to keep going in the face of adversity and defeat is always backed by hope.

As compared to hope, which could be passive, optimism is more active and is backed by determination. *If hope is about floating, optimism is about swimming.*

Hope and optimism means having strong expectations with positive results. These emotional traits help in perseverance and bring in resilience.

Optimism is a great motivator. Optimists often make efforts to counter failure, as it comes. They don't blame themselves for the failure but look for other reasons to blame it on. Pessimists blame themselves for failure and look at it on a personal level – personal deficiency, they also feel that nothing can be done to reverse the situation and give up. Optimists always give things a fresh try with a new plan of action.

What you can hope for and what you can't, is what emotional intelligence is about.

'God grant me the serenity to
Accept the things I cannot change,
Courage to change the things I can,
And the wisdom to know the difference.'

– Dr Reinhold Niebuhr

During a momentous battle, a Japanese General decided to go on the offensive and attack even though his army was greatly outnumbered by enemy troops. He was confident that they would win, but his men were filled with doubt. On their way to the battle, they stopped at a religious shrine. After praying with his men, the General took out a coin and said, 'I shall now toss this coin. If it is heads, we shall win. If tails, we shall lose. Destiny will now reveal itself.'

He threw the coin into the air and all watched intently as it landed. It was heads. The soldiers were so overjoyed and filled with confidence that they vigorously attacked the enemy and emerged victorious. After the battle, a lieutenant remarked to the General, 'No one can change destiny.'

'Quite right,' the General replied as he showed the lieutenant the coin, which had heads on both sides.

The moral of the story is that, there is nothing like the power of optimism and positive thinking. It's a power much greater than one's own self.

Taking Criticism Positively

Taking an open and candid feedback about yourself, your work, your strengths and weaknesses, requires a big heart and a lot of courage. Many great leaders have the ability to review their performance and improve upon themselves by taking feedback from their peers as well as subordinates. There are many great actors who have gone on record to say that their wives were their greatest critics. **It makes a lot of sense to listen to others, especially those who work closely with you and see you on a day-to-day basis.** It helps those who sit on an ivory tower and think of themselves as being the best. Self-confidence is very important for success, but being foolhardy about your own capabilities and performances is the most dangerous of things to happen.

Many of us cannot take criticism and can become quite cynical about it. If you don't take criticism positively and continue to live in your 'makebelieve' world, you can never improve.

Make sure that you develop this habit of taking a feedback from time to time. It may often shake you up, but most of the time it will wake you up – much before you actually fail or disaster strikes. **Working on your drawbacks, based on an open feedback is the ability which also reflects a strong character and is a sure sign of a winner all the way.**

Taking personal criticism and sometimes cracking a joke on yourself are the signs of a towering personality.

'Courage is what it takes to stand up and speak. Courage is also what it takes to sit down and listen.'

– Winston Churchill

Humour is Contagious

One of the most contagious of positive emotions is humour. It can do wonders to a person, to a relationship and to the environment. Somewhere down the line in this hurly-burly of life, we have forgotten how to laugh – taking life too seriously. **Remember, a smile is an inexpensive way to improve your looks.**

A good sense of humour increases your efficiency and adds to the productivity of an organisation. At the personal level, it releases tension and adds that 'fizz' that has become extremely important in this service-based type of economic environment.

In the typical industry-based environment of yesteryears, laughter and humour were considered to be counter-productive. At work, you've got to be serious, look serious and behave seriously, otherwise you are not serious about the job. Get it? This was the ethos. In the 1940s, laughter was taboo in many companies. A plant manager lost his job in the Ford Motor Company because he was caught smiling on the job! This was almost as if he was stealing.

Use your sense of humour at the presentations, at appropriate moments and it can work wonders. Use it in lectures and talks, and it can keep people riveted to the speaker. I have seen a number of orators and prolific speakers use this skill of bringing humour in, leaving the audience thrilled, invigorated and thoroughly charged. Use it during interviews – but subtly and it works positively. It has been seen that candidates who make the interviewer smile once or twice during the interview, have a better chance of getting the job than those who sit with a glum face in front of the interviewing panel. Use humour during a heated argument and help it diffuse the situation. Use it often and it can prevent a burnout. Use it in the social environment and you will definitely become popular, sought-after and likeable. Who wants to spend an evening with a moron when they have an option to do so with a cheerful person? **Never ever attempt humour at someone else's cost. Laughing at someone, making fun of someone is emotional intelligence at its worst. It can hurt people and break relationships. It also projects you in poor light.**

Remember, it doesn't cost money, but wins friends, goodwill and adds fizz to life.

I would also like to add that in today's tough world, it is important to have hobbies and games as an essential part of your survival kit. Going for walks, treks, family outings, movies, games, singing and dancing are extremely important for a healthy emotional life.

You also must know where to apply the brakes when the going gets too hot under the collar. While chasing our work and life, we often forget that we need to take a break. It is also important for those who are in responsible positions, to understand that others need a break too.

I had a boss, who saw me getting worked up during the day. He observed my behaviour for a few days and one day called me and said, 'You had better go on leave.' I told him that I didn't want to go on leave because there was no need to do so. He then explained to me that I needed a break to unwind. I went on a break for a few days and it did do a lot of good to me. Once when I returned to work, I was at peace, totally charged and raring to go.

How many of us do this as bosses and how many of us realise this at a personal level?

Remember that fun and laughter are great healers and soothers for all of us.

Compassion

Those who think with their heads and not with their hearts, consider compassion to be a sign of weakness. They look at things, situations and people in the most matter-of-fact manner and presume that there is no room for emotions in the logical, competitive and analytical world of today. They are afraid that showing mercy may project them as being weak or timid.

Compassion, on the contrary, requires a large heart. *To forgive and forget is a leader's trait and a winner's attitude.* It wins you respect and unconditional loyalty from others. Whether it is the *Bhagwad Gita*, the *Bible* or the discourses of Lord Gautam Buddha – compassion has been taught by every religious text. People who show compassion, also tend to show grace under pressure. They never blame others for their own failures and take responsibility for whatever they do. They are, in fact, on a higher emotional plane than others. **But compassion is not the forte of sages alone – it can be the strength of an ordinary mortal as well. Compassion can transform people and provide that healing touch.** In order to put it into practise, it takes emotional maturity, experience and expertise to handle people and assess situations in their entirety. Let me tell you that even in today's materialistic world, you can show compassion and yet live effectively. People respond to compassion because that too, is a basic instinct.

It sometimes becomes difficult to take a decision between showing compassion or going the other way. **Listening to your heart may be a better bet in such situations. Don't forget – taking a harsh decision is always the easiest option.**

> *'It ain't those parts of the Bible that*
> *I can't understand that bother me.*
> *It is the parts that I do understand.'*
>
> – Mark Twain

The Emotional Impact of Cultures

The cultures of organisations have a profound emotional impact on their people. Schools, colleges, good companies, good regiments in the armed forces and even countries have strong cultures built over a period of time.

People identify themselves with the organisations that they belong to. This sense of belonging becomes the most important factor for an organisational culture to spread and to be sustained.

A student who makes it to a good business school, attends a semester for six months and returns home, bubbling with confidence, sure of himself. Although there is a value addition through the good curriculum, the major reason for this confidence is that he feels he is a part of an elite group, belonging to an elite organisation.

Schools and colleges that organise regular alumni meets inculcate the feeling, 'You are still a part of us.' **All over the world, regiments in the armed forces celebrate reunions and raising days to create that emotional bond between the old and the new. These are often nostalgic get-togethers with strong emotional feelings being aroused**. In a country as vast as India, an army personnel who walks into any cantonment feels absolutely secure and at home. He knows that he would be greeted with warmth and would be looked after. These traditions and cultures are those emotional bonds that motivate people to bring in injured comrades from minefields, run through a barrage of fire to help others, keep the flag of their regiments flying high and even make the supreme sacrifice. **If business organisations can build such trust and a sense of belonging even to a little extent, it would generate phenomenal organisational energy that would boost productivity. This, in the truest sense of the term, is applied Emotional Intelligence.** The armed forces can generate this sense of belonging and caring within the organisation, because of two basic reasons. The first and the foremost is to create a sense of pride in each individual about his own regiment. In addition to this, a lot of stress is given to participating in group activities. Organisations that want to create this sense of belonging must take the two approaches seriously. One may not achieve the levels of camaraderie and sacrifice as in the armed forces, but even a fraction of that, if achieved can work wonders.

Armed forces personnel the world over, are conscious of the fact that they are the ones who protect their countrymen and the sovereignty of the country that they belong to. This becomes a very major motivating factor. **NGOs that pay as little as 25 per cent of corporate salaries derive much higher levels of motivation from their employees than the corporate world, because they work for a cause.**

Similarly, organisational mission, vision and stance must clearly demonstrate that each employee contributes to society directly or indirectly, by working for organisational goals.

A pharmaceutical company, for example, must make each employee understand that he is providing that 'healing touch' to society by working for an organisation that manufactures medicine. This brings in a sense of purpose – which motivates people at an emotional, not at a materialistic level.

This also helps increase the overall Emotional Intelligence level in organisations. This is a slow, but surer method of increasing motivational levels in organisations. These methods also ensure employee commitment on a long-term basis.

Modest Pretensions

Great achievers are proud of their success, and why not? You work for it, you achieve it and you are proud of it. **You must be proud of what you do and you must take pride in what you do. After all, that is the basis of motivation for all of us. People go grossly wrong, when they mix up pride and arrogance.**

Ego and arrogance go hand-in-hand. People with an inflated ego, tend to boast about their achievements and try to show others down. They want to look big by making other people look small. As a result, whatever they achieve, goes down the drain because of an arrogant attitude. Those who are arrogant, are scoffed at by people and those who boast, often become a laughing stock.

Remember, your achievements are always seen and appreciated by your peers, subordinates, as well as friends. You don't have to make a big noise about these. To be humble, unassuming and proud of what you are is the sign of a great personality and a strong character. Many great achievers and personalities are humble and unassuming.

Real achievers in fact, are humble and that adds to their greatness. These people are approachable, friendly, forthcoming and above all, appreciate the achievements of others.

As far as managing emotions is concerned, this is, I think,

one of the easiest things to do. **This is also an impulse of sorts – an impulse to blow you trumpet, which is often out of tune. If you feel that you are not humble by nature, then you can at least pose that you are humble – and that is what matters.** If you stop bragging about yourself – be rest assured that you will be much more respected than what you are at present. Being humble means knowing your true position and abilities and yet not talking about these.

> *'They are proud in humility, proud in that they are not proud.'*
>
> – Robert Burton

IN A NUTSHELL

Emotions are at the centre of our existence. Our basic instincts developed in the form of emotions, which equipped us to survive and handle situations through evolution. The sixth sense, the gut feeling to see beyond the obvious and the tenacity to conquer failure are the gifts that make us progress as a race. As life became more organised, apart from our basic emotions for survival, other emotional competencies developed in order to make life more meaningful, richer and fuller. Therefore, many emotional strands go into making the positive emotional outlook. These emotions in today's modern society have become the basic ingredients for our success. Such is the power of these ingredients, that if we pay adequate attention to improve upon them, even in small proportions, it will make a big difference to the quality of our life.

For example, people who are prepared to wait for rewards and work patiently to achieve what they want, have always done better than those who resort to short-cuts and an 'easy way out.' They also develop into better people, contribute more to society and the environment in general.

Good performers in any arena have that single-mindedness and the ability to totally be immersed in whatever they do. They are in a state of ecstacy and in perfect flow with their job at hand – which makes them winners all the way.

Then there are characteristics like caring for others, charity and compassion, that go a long way in the making of a human being, a good person, a good citizen and a good worker. Nature has also given us feelings like optimism and hope, that allow us to work towards a goal with a positive frame of mind. God gave us humour to bring a little fun and happiness into our lives. It is a great soother, which can wash off all the tension accumulated during the day. It can help make good relations and even diffuse difficult and tricky situations.

God has also given us the courage and serenity to take criticism from others. If taken positively, this acts as a very good feedback mechanism to review our performance at the workplace, as well as at home. Nature has also infused in us (at least in some of us) that quality of being humble, despite our great achievements. All these positive traits put together, reflect a good character, a strong personality and the right attitude, that lead us to success.

The art of soothing ourselves is a fundamental life skill.

Your Personal Road Map

1. List some charitable actions that you have undertaken in your life.

2. From now onwards, while dealing with people, put yourself in their shoes to understand their genuine feelings.

3. Promise yourself that you will not be sarcastic with anyone at home or at work.

4. Try to develop a more caring attitude towards others and try finding positive things in people around you.

5. Try and develop a sense of pride by setting higher goals and achieving them.

6. Write down three simple ways through which you can improve the ability of delayed gratification in yourself.

7. Try inculcating the habit of taking criticism positively at home as well as at work. Remember, this would boost your self-esteem and others will respect you for this.

8. Make a deliberate effort to bring humour into your home, social circle and workplace. Remember, it will win you friends, goodwill and will pep up your life.

9. Promise yourself to show compassion while dealing with people.

10. Promise not to blow your own trumpet or be arrogant with people. Remember, being humble earns you respect and appreciation from your bosses, peers as well as subordinates.

4

Attitudes, Temperaments and Success:

The Great Men

'At the performance level of humans, Chemistry is more important than Physics.'

THE IMPORTANCE OF RIGHT ATTITUDE

The direction of the flight of a rocket in technical terms, is known as its 'attitude.' If the attitude changes only by a few degrees, the rocket will fall into the Arabian Sea instead of going on course and reaching its target. As a thumb rule, if the destination is farther, the error is also larger – even for a small error in attitude.

For us, aptitude is a set of skills to do things, whereas attitude is the will to do things. A positive attitude also means viewing things positively. You may have a very high Intelligence Quotient, a logical mind backed with great education and training. But if you don't have that will to do things and put your skills to work, all other skills are rendered useless. You will be like a misdirected rocket – reaching the wrong destination. Remember, the journey of life is fairly long and our destination is far away. A small error in attitude can ensure that we will never be able to reach our destination. **Make a small change in your attitude and I guarantee you the shortest and surest path to success – which is everyone's dream destination.**

Also remember, it is not the altitude, but the attitude which takes you to the right destination. **It is not important how high you fly, but it is important where you fly to.**

Keep your feet firmly on ground and look for the right direction. JRD Tata put it differently. He said that one word that can make all the difference is 'attitude', because on an alphabetic scale of 1 to 26, A at 1 and Z standing at 26, the sum of the letters ATTITUDE is a perfect hundred! And I say, so is DISCIPLINE. Check it out.

I have seen that toppers in the best business schools do not get the best jobs during campus recruitment programmes. The best jobs are for those who have that positive attitude – that fire in the belly, that grit, that attitude to set high targets for themselves and get a high while achieving these. **A small difference lies in the attitude, but the big difference lies in the fact whether it is positive or negative.**

Film directors and co-stars of Shahrukh Khan say that even after giving his best shot in front of the camera, he wants to make another attempt to improve. He competes with himself and *that* is the biggest competition – a matter of attitude. That is the secret of his success. **A hundred meter sprinter practices everyday on the track. He then competes only with himself.**

Everyday he wants to beat himself by clocking a better timing. It is the thrill of achievement and the sense of achievement, which becomes the greatest motivator for achieving. Make it a habit to break your own records – however small – and you will start respecting yourself more and more. This is self-esteem in its simplest form.

A bad attitude not only reduces your output, but also negatively influences people around you, your work place, your friends and family. A positive attitude enhances your own performance as well as of those who are around you. It has that ripple effect in teams and organisations. It is infectious.

Harry Sandhu is a friend of mine, who flies helicopters. A pilot by profession, he narrates a small incidence. Long ago as a co-pilot, while flying at an altitude of 15,000 feet, his helicopter developed a technical snag. It was an emergency, and the cockpit was charged with panic and fear. The captain of the helicopter was ready for an emergency landing. Apart from handling his part of the job in an emergency landing drill, Harry kept telling the Captain, 'Sir, don't worry, we will land safely.' He kept saying, 'It is a matter of minutes and we will be landing safely.' This positive talk did a lot of good and they did land safely. The Captain of the helicopter gave him the credit and said, 'We are alive today because of your positive inputs – had you panicked, we would have never lived to see this day again.' This is the power of thinking positively and giving a positive feedback. An overall positive outlook is important for success and survival. **Companies hire people on skill and fire them because of their attitudes.**

Attitude in brief, affects and influences your performance in the following major areas:

- Interpersonal skills
- On-the-job success
- Physical health
- The physical performance of athletes, output of musicians, painters and artists.
- Your overall well-being

People with positive attitude not only succeed, they have the spirit to fight all odds. With a sheer positive outlook, people have conquered illness, disease and failure. **These are the bosses whom you go to, when your chips are down. These are the friends who you like to share your problems with, who are always ready to give you right advice and support. These are the peers who can infuse confidence in you when you are in a difficult situation.**

"It is not enough to just do your job. If you have a negative impact on other people around you, you are a liability."

Then, there are people who look at things – and as a matter of fact at life – negatively. They are a part of the problem and not the solution. They will always tell you how things can't be done. They are pessimists, for whom glass is always half-empty and never half-full. They are the perpetual blamers. These are the bosses who never inspire confidence. They are those friends whom you avoid. They are the peers you could never bank on for a positive boost. You better look at yourself – an honest look – and the type of person that you are. Also, evaluate how others look at you. **If you have a problem with your attitude and you accept it, I bet you have won more than half the battle.**

Having done that, make deliberate efforts to look at things positively. Remember, it is you who has to make the efforts for this change. It is your attitude, after all. You have to have an attitude towards changing your attitude if you want to change it.

"You can take a horse to the water and make him drink. But if you take an ass to the water you can't make him drink."

Temperament

The sum total of emotions, reactions and feelings is temperament. Each one of us is born with a temperament. It is difficult to change it, but not impossible to do so. **I would like to emphasise that you cannot transform but you can always tame.**

'Men acquire a particular quality by constantly acting in a particular way . . . you become just by performing just actions, temperate by performing

temperate actions and brave by performing brave actions.'

– Aristotle

You've got to have patience and perseverance to bring about a gradual change in yourself.

The Doberman and the Pomeranian are two breeds of dogs, that are temperamentally aggressive and snappy. A lot depends on the master, on how he trains them, tames them and rears them. If brought up in a friendly and loving home, these dogs can become friendly and loving. We have all seen whales being trained. We have seen cases where convicts shun crime. All I am trying to say is that if animals can change and if hard core criminals can be changed, then why can't we make an effort to change those minor temperamental nuances that become a hurdle to our day-to-day living, that contribute negatively to our progress and success. **It is easy to change 1 per cent in 100 areas, than trying to change 100 per cent in one area.**

Therefore, take these problems in small piece-meals – taking them on slowly, but surely.

There was an old blind man who used to draw his pension from a bank. Since he was blind, his nephew used to come along with him to assist him. The cashier would hand over the cash to the old man, who after counting the money would give it to his nephew in order to check it once more. In the bargain, the boy would pocket Rs 300 and quietly return the balance to the blind man. This went on for sometime, but one day the cashier couldn't resist himself and went and told the old man how he was being duped by this young boy. The old man was not surprised and told the cashier that he knew what his nephew was doing all the while, but was keeping quiet on purpose. He said, after all the boy was nice to him, looked after him and was ready to accompany him to the bank every month. The episode, therefore, continued. When the old man died, to the cashier's surprise he had bequeathed his entire property to this young nephew. After a decade or so, this cashier learnt that the young man was now a teacher in a school. 'What kind of morals will this chap teach to the children?' he thought. So, he went to the school one day, to find out the state of affairs.

He was shocked to find that this boy not only turned out to be a good and a dedicated teacher, he had even donated half of his inherited property to build an orphanage!

The moral of the story is that a person can change himself. If a person has a negative or a bad habit, he need not be condemned for life. There is always room for improvement.

'Habit is a habit and not to be flung out of the window by any man, but coaxed downstairs, a step at a time.'

– Mark Twain

GREAT MEN

Temperament and attitude are the broad indicators of a person's traits. As I mentioned earlier, winners compete against themselves. They set high targets and work hard to achieve them – in fact they love what they do.

People who are not only winners, but qualify to be called 'Great Men', are those who make a difference with a dream and an attitude.

'Great Men – whether great social reformers, great thinkers, statesmen, sages, patriots or men of letters – differ from common men only in one thing: they have the courage to dream and also work to turn it into reality. They give life a meaning, a purpose and dedicate themselves to that purpose.

The truly great are not the men of wealth and possession, not men who gain name and fame, but those who testify to the truth in them and refuse to compromise, whatever be the costs.

They are determined to do what they consider to be right. We may punish their bodies, refuse their comforts, but we cannot buy their souls, we cannot break their spirits.

Whosoever possesses this invulnerability of spirit, even to a little extent deserves our admiration.'

– S Radhakrishnan

The above statement is by Dr S Radha Krishnan, a great philosopher and erstwhile President of the Republic of India. This, to many, may appear as a theoretical piece of wisdom, but let me tell you that it is true to its every word. It talks of people who have the courage to dream and more importantly, those, who work for their dream. It is about those who give a meaning to their existence and refuse to compromise. People who are spirited and stand by their high values. Pick up the example of any Great Man – who you consider great – by your standards and yardstick. Somewhere deep down, you will find some of these qualities in your Great Men. This statement, in fact, sums up Emotional Intelligence – at least all of its major aspects.

Goals and Dreams

Try to recollect a dream that you had last night. You may possibly recollect it, but it will always be hazy – shrouded in mist. In a dream, it rains and shines. You could be sitting on a hilltop in broad daylight, looking at the moon! **Dreams are never very clear. They are often foggy, misty, frosty and yet vivid. People who dream about what they want to achieve, also do not have an absolutely clear vision. They can, however, see the broad direction through the fog.** A glimpse of the view beyond the fog becomes the driving force for them, which sometimes becomes a mission in life. Then, they work to make that dream come true. They are prepared to cross that fog even if it means taking risk.

Intangible Goals are Loftier than Tangible Goals

Most of the achievers do not quantify their ultimate goals – because the ultimate is neither quantifiable nor achievable. They keep working hard and many of them leave a legacy behind, a *virasat*, a trail of achievements. Remember, if you quantify a goal in numbers, you are automatically putting a cap on your achievements, for example, 1 million is 1 million and no more.

Great Men set out to achieve great tasks, without actually quantifying their goals. Many times their goals and dreams are very simple and innocent. These are the goals of the heart and not the head. When they start, they have very little in their hands but they have a flame in their hearts – which becomes 'Amar Joyti' and they make sure that the flame never dies down.

One such dreamer was Rippan Kapur, who started the legendry organisation, Child Relief and You, popularly known as CRY. A flight purser with an airline, with a well-paid job, Rippan wanted to help under-privileged children who didn't have anyone to help them. When he quit his job to start this organisation, people thought he was crazy. Friends advised him against it. Relatives resisted it. But, Rippan had a dream, he had a mission. He had Rs 50 in hand, a flame in his heart and nothing else. His mother was the only one who backed him and he was in a world of his own – a dream – a trance. **He started alone, but was a firm believer, that if people get together for a cause, they can make a difference.**

In the beginning, he started single-handedly with an idea and launched his mission in 1979, supported by six friends, each one, chipping in seven rupees. He did all kinds of odd jobs for the organisation, himself. Today, 23 years later, the organisation has made a profound difference to more than 1 million children in India and has involved 100,000 individuals and organisations in its movement.

CRY is living proof that when enough people can be made to believe that change is possible – it becomes possible. Belief can start a movement. It also proves

the power of the individual to create change. Rippan is no more – but his fervour, his vision and his relentless positive energy that drove CRY is still alive. So, have a big dream and work to achieve it – it is possible.

'If we did all the things we were capable of doing we would literally astound ourselves.'

– Thomas Alva Edison

Another dreamer with a mission is Dr SB Mujumdar, the founder of Symbiosis – now a well-established, internationally recognised educational organisation. A Professor of Botany at Fergusson College, Pune, he as a rector realised that foreign students from developing nations studying in Pune, faced numerous difficulties. He wanted to create an organisation, which could be a home away from home for these foreigners who were aliens in our country. He also wanted to help them in their learning process. With this attitude of helping those who needed help, he started a small educational organisation. He started with a mission of quality education and caring for others in the late 1970s. His dream of quality education, is today a university with more than 26,000 students on campus, in 28 wonderful institutions. The word 'symbiosis' a botanical term for living together for mutual benefit, says it all about his philosophy – live in harmony. He had a dream, which he believed in, he had a comfortable job, which he left to pursue his dream. **With a flame in his heart and a dream in his head, he set out without quantifying his goals and has achieved something that all of us would be envious of.**

India is today, the largest producer of milk in the world. Thanks to Dr Verghese Kurien, the father of the White Revolution and architect of Operation Flood. Starting his career as a dairy engineer in a government creamery at Anand, a small town in Gujarat in 1949, he volunteered to help an infant farmers' cooperative dairy organisation, which was fighting a battle with Polson, a privately-owned dairy for market share. He wanted the farmers to get a fair deal for their produce. He was also looking for a challenge in his profession, which his government job failed to offer him. He found happiness by serving dairy farmers in Gujarat – in retrospect, he says that the happiness which he caught 50 years ago was infectious and never left Anand thereafter. He wanted dairy farmers of Gujarat to be the owners of the business. He created the Anand Milk Union Limited – popularly known as AMUL dairy products. With his determination, he could mobilise 2 million farmers in Gujarat and motivate an organisation to produce world-class products. He made such a huge success of his mission that his 'Amul pattern' of cooperatives was replicated across India as the National Dairy Development Board. His mission was – the development of farmers, nutrition to the nation, and at the core of it, development of rural India.

His was the largest rural employment programme in the country, trebling the nation's milk production within a span of two-and-a-half decades. This made India the largest producer of milk in the world, giving the US a run for its money. Remember, he had a dream – a big dream – but he didn't know how big it was, till it materialised.

Think big, dream big, commit to your purpose from your heart and motivate others to commit, says Dr Kurien. He also asks you to listen to words of wisdom, no matter which quarter they come from, and be downright honest. These are the golden thoughts of a humble dreamer. Most of such achievers, when they look back, would say, 'I never knew that I could achieve this much.' Most achievers, in fact, don't dream of money. They do not crave for money – they crave for something else, which eventually, also brings in money. Money becomes a by-product.

If the founder of a software company says, 'I want to make the best operating system in the world and that is my dream', he would be a greater achiever, than if he said that his dream is a $200 million company. The former, being an intangible goal, and the latter, being a limited, quantifiable achievement. Therefore, in order to aspire to be the best in your field or whatever you do, will be a much loftier goal than mere numbers, dollars or rupees. As Shahrukh Khan says, 'If you can dream it, you can achieve it.' Dream with a sparkle in your eye and a flame in your heart – this is a sure recipe for success. Don't get things wrong. Dreaming does not mean that you have no plans, no perceptions, no achievable, definable goals. Yes, you do. Small targets are achievements at a tactical level to go along with and finally realise that dream. All those who dream, plan their daily schedules, their monthly targets and their annual goals. The difference is, they think big and work smart.

Stretching Yourself a Little

When John F Kennedy went to school, they played a game, which became popular with kids. The boys had to go around the barn crossing fences, brooks and walls and the one who finished earliest, was the winner. They would often come up against a difficult obstacle and be very scared of crossing it – but would eventually find a simple method to go across such tough hindrances. To accomplish this, they would all throw their hats across the obstacle that seemed invincible. Now, since their hats were already across, there was no choice but to go across the obstacles and fetch those! So they went along and crossed it. People commit themselves beforehand, so that they have to honour their commitments. This is a good way of stretching yourself a little to go that extra mile.

Early Impressions

Rabindranath Tagore classified the age of 14 years as a 'tender' age. This is the time during our lives, when we are most impressionable. Therefore, the philosophy, the world over, is to 'catch them young.' Indoctrination is best done at an early age. What we see at home, learn at school and from the company we keep during our school days, goes a long way. It in fact, influences us almost all our lives. Mr Sam Pitroda, Chairman, WorldCom who, was on our campus said, 'The die is cast by the time that you are 10 or 12 years old.' What you learn from your parents, teachers and friends is also called *'sanskar'*, or the quality of righteous living. **If a child sees that his parents are liars, cheats and tricksters, chances are**

that he will acquire these traits during his childhood, practice them as he grows and master them by the time that he matures. Learning good habits, imbibing value systems – that are a part of developing Emotional Intelligence – are most affectively carried out when we are children. Caring, compassion, charity, modesty and honesty is learnt at an early age. In order to build a good nation and a good society, we need to reach out to our kids when they are young and when their minds are impressionable and receptive. **Each one of us will do a great favour, to our families, society and our country if we take on the responsibility of initiating good values even for one young person at home or anywhere in society.** When you do this, you pave the way for making Great Men out of ordinary people.

'Always do right. It will gratify some people and astonish the rest.'

– Mark Twain

Honesty and Integrity

These sound old-fashioned, but these qualities are universally accepted as star qualities. **Would you like to hire a person, whose integrity is questionable, even as a peon? Would you like to deal with a peer who has dubious integrity?** The answer is a big 'NO.' We all expect others to be honest, but often falter, when it comes to personal integrity. **Let me also tell you that there are lots of honest people and they also live equally well – mostly better than the dishonest ones.** The truth is, it is possible to be honest and live well. Honesty has nothing to do with how much money you have, or how well-positioned you are in the hierarchy, or how well-placed you are in the society. *Honesty is an attitude.* I have seen people who draw a salary of Rs 3,000 a month, being honest. I have also seen people earn Rs 3 lakh per month and behave dishonestly. It is all in one's mind! People involved in scams have enough to eat, maybe more than enough, but they are, unfortunately, extremely dissatisfied. That's the difference!

A friend of mine went to pay his electricity bill. The bill amounted to Rs 780, but he handed over two notes of Rs 500 each, as he didn't have change. There was a lot of rush at the counter and a long queue behind him which forced him to quickly collect his receipt from the counter clerk, forgoing his balance. He had to rush back to work, and so he started quickly towards his car. He was surprised by a tap on his shoulder. The counter clerk had come running behind him to return Rs 220.

The moral of the story is that, the league of honest people also consists of poor citizens, whose poverty does not make them succumb to dishonest means. This is why, we are still surviving as humankind. This tribe of honest people, however, is fast-depleting. In a lighter vein they are the 'endangered species.'

The Golden Catch

There was a young boy, about 12 years of age, who went fishing with his father. They reached the fishing site quite early and the boy started practicing casting with his fishing rod. Suddenly, he caught a huge fish – both of them were amazed at such a big catch. The boy was thrilled to bits. But his father looked at his watch and saw that, it was 4.00 pm, two hours before the official time of fishing started. His father said, 'You will have to put it back son.' No one was watching them, there were no boats, no officials or people around. The boy protested, but he knew from his father's tone that the order was non- negotiable. He did as he was told. 35 years later, the boy grew up to be a very successful businessman. He still remembers that incident.

He could never catch that big a fish ever, but remembered that fish again and again whenever a question of ethics came up. He learnt honesty when he was young and practiced it when he matured.

The moral of the story is that, ethics is a simple matter of right and wrong. Practicing it is very difficult. Can we do the right things when nobody is looking at us? We would, if we would have been taught to put the fish back into the river, when we were young.

'God could not be everywhere, and so he made mothers.'

– A Jewish Proverb

Ethics and honesty, as well as integrity are non-negotiable. Also, they are either there, or not there. You are either honest or you are dishonest. **A women can either be pregnant or not pregnant. She can't be 'somewhat' pregnant!**

Role Models

A role model is someone whom you look up to. You hold such people in high esteem and they act as a beacon to give you a broad direction in life. Role models need not necessarily be celebrities, industrialists, or heads of states. In most of my interactive sessions, I ask the participants to spell out who their role models are. Many people find their role models in their dads, grandmothers, elder brothers or even a neighbour next door. These are the people whom you respect, admire, appreciate and would like to emulate. When I ask the participants to list the qualities of their role models, they bring out very simple human qualities, that they appreciate in their role models. Somebody would say, 'My dad is my role model because he is very honest and has given us a good upbringing, despite his meagre resources.' Many people find their role models in those who have bounced back after a number of setbacks. Then there are role models who are humble, unassuming, simple people. Role models are those who care for others and have contributed to society. They are those who have achieved something big with minimal resources. Then, there are people who find role models in great engineers, scientists, finance buffs or successful entrepreneurs – they are, however, very few in number. Even entrepreneurs and inventors are appreciated for their basic qualities of grit and determination. **People appreciate Thomas Alva Edison for his tenacity of trying 999 times before he could successfully make a bulb – and maybe not because he invented the bulb!** These are the qualities of Great Men and you appreciate these very 'simple qualities' that make them great.

'We are, what we repeatedly do.'

– Aristotle

I am trying to drive home the fact that we look up to people who have these basic human qualities of caring for others, giving back to society, handling failures, honesty, grit, simplicity and determination to name a few. Don't you think that we should acquire and demonstrate such qualities at home, at work or in society at large, so that people can look up to us? Whether it is the boy next door, corporate honchos like Narayana Murthy, Jack Welch or leaders like Winston Churchill and Nelson Mandela – we appreciate them all because of their basic virtues – of Emotional Intelligence. You need not have only one role model. Pick up all the positive qualities from those who have these strengths and try to infuse them into your personality, and into your being. Remember, you want to become like them.

Success and Satisfaction

Success means different things for different people. Success, satisfaction and happiness are very closely, if not directly linked. Money, position, power and fame are all essentials for a meaningful life. All of us can't be saints and sages. It is not even essential. It is at the same time, important to understand what satisfies you – what you want out of life.

'It is the nature of desire not to be satisfied, and most men live only for the gratification of it.'

– Aristotle

Success and satisfaction has to be seen from three angles. One's job, home and society. People very often link success and satisfaction only to the job that they do – missing out on the big picture. Further, they view success at their workplace, only in terms of the pay packet and their position in the hierarchy – often ignoring the most important components – satisfaction and happiness.

I have a friend who works for an old age home. I think he is doing a great service, a good job. But surprisingly, he has very often told me that he is waiting to retire. He has a well-paid job, but he seems to be unhappy. It is a great job but it gives him no satisfaction. **Remember, we work for a large part of our lives, and after we retire, there is very little left in terms of time or what really matters. If you are eagerly waiting for your retirement, so that you can hang up your boots – then you are not satisfied with what you are doing.**

While interacting with the Chairman of WorldCom, Mr Sam Pitroda, at our Campus, a bright, young boy asked him, 'Sir, how would you like to define your success?' He was probably expecting an answer from a successful corporate in dollars or dimes.

Sam Pitroda gave a simple matter-of-fact reply, 'I have two children who stay with me in the US. They respect my wife and me and discuss everything that they do and would like to do in life with us. And that is my success.'

This is not philosophy – This is life.

If you listen to your heart and find out what satisfies you – you would be content. The most important thing

is to have the courage to follow your heart, if you want to join the league of extraordinary great men.

As I had said earlier, role models are people who you would like to emulate. They are 'direction finders.' If you are lost in a desert or a jungle, a compass or the Pole Star shows you the direction. In our life, we need to take the right direction – and need role models to help us find that direction.

In a much broader sense, the core values dictate what you want and what you should do. Great men hold on tightly to their core values, be it Rippan Kapur, Verghese Kurien or Dr Mujumdar – tomorrow, it could very well be you.

IN A NUTSHELL

People with great education and absolutely brilliant brains can fail in life because of their wrong attitude. Those with the right attitude find something good, something personal in everything that they come across. However, those with the wrong attitude will always find something wrong in everything even if it is right. Attitude effects not only your own performance, it also has a profound effect on the attitude of people around you. Therefore, in order to be successful and happy at work, in the social environment and at home, it is very important to have a positive attitude. We all inherit a temperament, which is sum total of our feelings and reactions. It dictates how we behave and is reflected in our overall personality. You can work on your temperament and make a positive change, which can help shape up your life better. Changing your attitude is possible as long as you make attempts to achieve things step-by-step.

People who have a positive attitude and also the ability to dream about something they want – are the real winners. They give a meaning to their lives and have the purpose and spirit to fight the odds to achieve that purpose. These great men don't really quantify their goals – they think with their hearts. With this attitude, they achieve what most of us are envious of.

It is also important to understand that we all learn things during our childhood and whatever we learn, last a lifetime. Attitudes, honesty and integrity are best learnt at home. As responsible citizens, we need to inculcate these habits and initiate good values for young minds at home as well as at school. In order to achieve goals, you must have benchmarks and some broad directions to follow. Role models help us in this regard. It is always good to look up to someone whom you admire and try to pick up the best out of such people, whom you would like to emulate.

Happiness, success and satisfaction at the end of the day, go hand-in-hand. There is no success if you are not happy and satisfied. Remember, satisfaction and happiness is equally important at home as well as at work.

'A great obstacle to happiness is to anticipate too great a happiness.'

– Fontanels

Your Personal Road Map

1. What is the importance of attitude and how do you improve it and make it positive?

2. Name three people who you think are successful. Why do you think they are successful?

3. What qualities would you like your partner, friend, employee and boss to possess?
   - Partner
   - Friend
   - Employee
   - Boss

   Tick those qualities, that are related to attitude.

4. List one simple factor that makes you proud of yourself.

5. What are the moral values and advice that you would like to give your children or juniors? List at least three of them.

6. Write down one incident which proves that you have a strong will power and perseverance.

7. Achievements that I am proud of:
   - Childhood
   - College
   - Work

8. List all the negative attributes of your temperament, that come in the way of your success at:
   - Home
   - Work
   - Social circle

9. What makes people successful?

10. Elucidate the moral values that you learnt during your childhood. Tick all those that you still possess.

5

Find Your Cup of Tea:

Passions, Potentials, Purpose and Perseverance

'Talent is what you possess; Genius is what possesses you.'

– Malcolm Cowley

YOUR LIKES AND DISLIKES

As we go along in life, we gradually come to know of our own temperament, our likes and dislikes, our own feelings and passions. We come to know what interests us and what excites us. Passion is a strong word, which describes a very strong feeling in us for any desire. But even if it is not passion, deep down, we all have some desires, strong affinities for certain things or certain activities. It is most important to 'listen' to these feelings and align one's activities and goals around these strong desires.

If your likes can be aligned with your profession, or more appropriately, if your profession can be aligned with your desires, you will get a real high in life. You will achieve what we so often describe in management parlance as job satisfaction. On the contrary, if you don't like your job, you will never be able to perform and be happy.

Look at MF Hussain, the great artist. He is equally excited when he paints a horse, a bull or Madhuri Dixit. He is the happiest person in the world with his paint, brush and canvas. Sachin Tendulkar and Tiger Woods, love their game and earn too! **If you love your work, you are on a permanent holiday.**

The same thing happens with actors, architects, doctors and designers. Those who love their work, out-perform others and certainly excel. Dev Anand, the octogenarian legend, still makes movies. He still has his boots on and is on the move, because he loves what he does. He still works more than 12 hours a day on his film projects. Passion gives him energy. So, you have to find what you like, find your cup of tea and then brew it the way you want, and rest assured, you will love it and you will succeed.

Climbing Down the Ladder

I had earlier mentioned that we are climbing ladders placed by others in front of us. Many of us do that and repent. We regret it throughout our lives. 'I wish I did what I wanted to,' we say, but go on doing what others advice us to do. Take others' advice, but listen to your heart as well.

I once met Shekhar Kapur, the legendary film director, way back in the year 1973. It was a chance meeting at Napean Sea Road, Mumbai, where I had gone to meet my brother who was fond of theatre and used to coach aspiring actors into its nuances. My brother's theatre was small and a number of boys and girls were practising and rehearsing their lines. I saw a young, fairly good-looking person of almost my age on the stage. Later, during the lunch break I was introduced to him and I learnt from him that he had finished his studies in London and had come to Mumbai to settle down. 'What had he studied?' I asked. It turned out that the person had not completed a course from the London School of Drama, but that he had done his Chartered Accountancy. I was shocked – what had this man done! I couldn't resist myself and asked him the reason behind his change of heart. After all, as a qualified Chartered Accountant, he could have got a good job or he could have started his own company.

His answer was, 'It is not my cup of tea.' I was amazed at this young man who must have spent a lot of time, money and effort to acquire a CA degree, which most of us would give our left arm for, and here he was, trying to switch over to something which was not even remotely connected with his experience and qualification. He tried his hand at acting, not with any spectacular success, but stuck to his guns, to become one of the most successful and respected film directors internationally. His talent and style has been recognised the world over, with films like *Masoom, The Bandit Queen* and *Elizabeth*. He is an icon and is currently working on his next mega project on Nelson Mandela. What else could he have asked for from life?

What Shekhar Kapur did, was to climb down the ladder, and that too, a golden one. He wanted to make a change, he knew what he liked and that it was different from what he was currently doing. Above all, he had the guts to climb down the ladder to find his cup of tea. Today, he is a successful and satisfied man. At a personal level, he would be more satisfied, than successful.

Anytime is Good Time

It is not necessary to find your strong likes at an early age. Many times, you discover what you like and what you are good at, much later in life. It can happen during your mid-twenties like in the case of Shekhar Kapur, or it could even happen in your mid-forties. Man's ability to uplift himself can develop at any moment in life. Whenever it comes, grab it, because this is how you grab your happiness. I have seen people turn to writing prose, poetry, teaching, meditation or an area of business that they like, quite late in life. Many would not dare to venture into such territory, because people already consider them to be on the other side of the hill. Many people foray into a venture, even after they retire from their run-of-the-mill job. The scope of these ventures is limited only by our imagination. Never consider yourself to be too old to chase your passion. Many young people today follow what I call the 'safety net approach.' They acquire a marketable qualification like an engineering degree, a degree in medicine and even an MBA and then venture out to find their 'cup of tea'. This is a very good and practical way to follow your heart, with your head firmly in place. This approach has the advantage that if things don't work out as you perceive them, you have a safe fallback option to make a decent living. Education and a fallback option gives you that additional confidence and courage which is required to change tracks.

I have no statistics to prove as to how many people do jobs that they don't like. They do it because they just have to. But I am sure, that there are a large number of people who do exist in such unhappy situations. They need to liberate themselves and move towards happier pastures. **The greatest tragedy I know of is that so many young people never discover what they really want to do. No one else, I think is to be pitied so much as the person who gets nothing at all out of his work, but his pay.**

Shekhar Suman, who has made it big on the small screen in recent years – his programmes being aired on seven TV channels simultaneously, is a successful man. He commands the highest price that a TV star ever did. His contract with Sony Entertainment Television, for a programme was for Rs 25 crore. A rival channel offered him Rs 100 crore to switch over – a four-fold jump and big money. Shekhar says he was lured by this offer because such opportunities don't come up very often. He thought it to be unethical and rung up his father for advice. His father asked him, 'Are you happy with what you are doing?' Shekhar said, 'Yes.' 'Are the people at Sony treating you badly?' He said, 'No.' Then don't take this offer, was the advice. Shekhar Suman dropped the offer and says, 'I am proud because I took the right decision – an ethical one.' He listened to his heart – doing what he liked and what he thought was right.

The Job Context

Money is important, but it is not the only factor for satisfaction. Many studies in Human Resource Management indicate that the job content, the job context and the environment are more important for retaining good people and getting them to work hard in organisations, than paying them fat salaries alone.

Remember, millionaires work the hardest, whereas they need not work at all. For them, the passion of hard work is more important than money. For them, work is enjoyment and relaxation.

Games are a good example of job context. Cricket is exciting because of the challenge that it poses, the uncertainty and the outcome of each ball being different. Variations in the pitch, the weather conditions, efforts made by the fielders, coordination of the batsmen and the way that each ball is delivered, creates excitement. The setting is so challenging, that it doesn't remain merely a game of hitting out at the ball with a bat. It becomes an exciting game because a context has been created.

Consider golf as a game. For an outsider, it could seem very boring. Putting balls into holes doesn't sound exciting at all. In a four to five hours' game, a player

swings only for three to four minutes! Then, what makes it exciting? It is the context. Fifty per cent of golf, they say, is about getting dressed – wearing the right shoes, the right cap, the right tee-shirt, a good bag, gloves, dark glasses, et al. Then there is challenge and a competition – you compete with yourself.

There are different clubs, different degrees of difficulty for each green, different distances and different obstacles on the way. Then there is variety, exercise, ambience, greenery, the pleasure of expanse, good company, socialisation and the satisfaction of playing a good game, scoring better than the last time. Golf also gives one the fun of immediate feedback and recognition.

Imagine such a boring activity of swinging at a ball being made so interesting by creating the right atmosphere and changing the context of the activity. Then why not bring such a change into your job too – think about it and it can be done.

The Moral Re-Armament Asia Plateau at Panchgani, Maharashtra, is an organisation dedicated to bringing good moral values back into society. They run residential programmes for professionals, executives, families and students. The unique thing about these programmes is the 'involvement of participants.' The schedule is hectic, but very refreshing. The entire service for breakfast, lunch and dinner is organised by the participants. Serving food, washing utensils and laying the tables is done as a team. Washing utensils for the whole batch is done by a small team of participants. The team works together, washing utensils while singing songs and cracking jokes. A number of basins are provided with hot water and soap, making it an assembly-line operation – with the last group wiping cutlery with towels to impart that sparkling-clean look. It is, in fact, so much fun washing utensils, that people volunteer to do it again and again! See, how they changed the context of the job by bringing in fun and providing a comfortable way of cleaning utensils? Such is the power of 'context.'

Going for a picnic is enjoyable, because of its very context. You have lunch everyday, but a lunch served and eaten with friends on a river bank or a hilltop after a long trek, far away from the crowds under the shade of trees is great fun. It is more exciting to eat what you carried on your backpack, rather than eating in a restaurant.

Talents and Hobbies

Looking for talent within yourself and others? Read on.

'A boy who collects a few butterflies is not necessarily a future lepidopterist, nor is the young coin collector destined for a place in high finance if a few coins are the extent of his collection. But when a hobby survives in the face of many obstacles, we can be sure it has the solid support of genuine talent.'

– Bernard Haldane

There are numerous examples, that can be cited to illustrate the fact that hobbies that survive, indicate a strong talent. Indian film actor Govinda has always liked dancing. He would dance whenever there was an occasion to dance. He would dance during the *Ganapati* festival, he would dance at neighbours' weddings, and he would dance whenever the music was on. He would dance because he wanted to dance. Taking this as a natural talent, he rose to become a good actor, a hero, a comedian and an entertainer loved by millions in India. **When hobbies become passions and serious professions, they become reason for spectacular success.**

Acharya Rajneesh, popularly known as Osho, was a teacher of philosophy at a college in Madhya Pradesh. His was the most attended class and students loved his style of delivery. He skilfully turned his delivery into discourse, which millions liked and made him a cult figure. He had the talent, a philosophy and he had the conviction – he connected these three together to achieve something, that very few can even imagine. He became Bhagwan Rajneesh. He could always have remained a professor of philosophy, making a good living, teaching students and deriving satisfaction from the job that he had. But he knew his potential and wanted to be different. Hence, he changed his track to touch the hearts of millions – leaving a legacy behind.

> *'Whatever you are by nature, keep to it; never desert your own line of talent. Be what nature intended you for and you will succeed; try anything else, you will be ten thousand times worse than nothing.'*
>
> – Sydney Smith

Mrs Indira Gandhi, the Prime Minister of India was once asked by a press reporter, 'How do you work for 18 hours a day, throughout the year without getting tired? And where do you get this energy from?' She quipped, 'I don't get tired because I love what I am doing.'

Marriages are made in heaven and so are jobs: in the hindsight of it

All marriages are not love marriages and all marriages are not successful. Arranged marriages could succeed or bomb and love marriages could bomb or succeed. Typically, in love marriages, it is passion that brings people together before the marriage, whereas in arranged marriages, you match parameters and let people live together and learn to make the best of it after the marriage. At the end of the day, marriages succeed, provided you make some adjustments, give some, take some, and look at the positives of the other person, and inject some excitement into life through creativity and innovation.

Similarly, if you don't fall for a profession passionately, you can still make it succeed. If you haven't found your soulmate in your job, you can find its positives, find some excitement or create some experiment, innovate and you do find things working out and the going, getting to be great. After all, it is no crime to work for a living. If you could get satisfaction along with making money, it is a workable solution. **Take a job that you like, or better start liking the job you take.** It is also important to understand the difference between love, infatuation or a crush. As love and passion go hand-in-hand, a crush and an infatuation belong to the same category. A crush, which is mistaken for everlasting love, could be a dangerous ground for a serious marriage proposal. Similarly, an infatuation, mistaken as deep passion for something and taken up as a serious profession, could also prove a misadventure. **Identifying what you like is, therefore, a serious business. You need to take a little time to think clearly and identify what you like.** At the end of this chapter, I have suggested four simple steps to identify your cup of tea.

We will now look at those major denominators which if aligned, can make you a successful and satisfied person.

The Four Great Ps of Success and Satisfaction

I call it the four ball of success and satisfaction. Take any successful and satisfied man, and you will find that he is strong on these four Ps. If a person has all these Ps strong, as well as aligned, he becomes a spectacular success. We will look at some of these people who had strong Ps and see how it works. These four Ps of success are:

- Passion – 'The greatest motivator.'
- Potential – 'Do you have it in you?'
- Purpose – 'What does it mean to you?'
- Perseverence – 'When the going gets tough, the tough get going.'

As you read along, identify your own strengths and map them onto these four Ps. We all have some strong as well as some weak Ps. Leverage your strengths and work on the Ps, that you need to make stronger. Passion and potential go hand-in-hand. It is natural to like something that you perform well. As a rule of the thumb, you will never like an activity, which you can't handle well. In the case of Jhumpa Lahiri – the Pulitzer Award winner –

it was sheer love for writing that brought her fame. She feels most relaxed and gets the greatest amount of joy by sitting alone in a room and imagining characters – and the rest flows like magic. She also means it when she says that she doesn't write for people, but for herself. A good cricketer in the making will always be able to connect the ball. He doesn't need the best bat, he can do it with a bamboo or even a walking stick! Because he has it in him – and he likes doing it. Adolf Hitler used oratory to find success, bringing Germany out of turmoil on his sheer ability to speak and convince the masses.

The First P

Passion – your greatest motivator

'Passions overwhelm reason – time and again.'

Those of you who have fallen in love, would agree that you could do anything for your sweetheart – go to any length for that person. You could wait, you could go hungry, you could even stand on one leg, you could defy the world, you could tolerate discomfort, heat, dust, and much more – just to be with your love. Love and passion for work, also operate in a similar manner and at a similar plane. Here, chemistry rules over physics! It is all in the mind.

> *'Mazdoor hath se kam karta hai, karigar hath our dimag se kam karta hai, . . . Kalakar hath, dimag our dil se kam karta hai.'*

The single winning factor for a *kalakar*, an artist is *dil se*. His heart is in his job. This is passion. Passion does work wonders in every field – because it sees no reasons. It works for sportsmen, artists, poets, designers, mountaineers, actors, engineers, scientists, doctors and any other worthwhile profession that you can think of. People with passion stand head above shoulders in a crowd. They are committed, dedicated and totally involved. They do it because they love doing it. In whatever they do, they transform themselves into a kalakar. Many times, they are fanatically in love with what they do.

The Second P

Potential: Do you have it in you?

Remember, each one of us can do two or three things better than at least 50,000 people. Find these strengths, use them to your advantage and you will be a better and more satisfied person in life.

Now this is the most important factor for satisfaction and success. Many times, we wonder what we are and what our strength is. We want to be someone, we want to do something, without having the natural talent or capability for that yearning. If one can dispassionately identify one's strengths and weaknesses, and then try to hone them – success and satisfaction will follow.

Adolf Hitler wanted to be an architect; he used to put lots of efforts into making blueprints and drawings. After World War I, when Germany was trying to find its feet, there was a lot of political discussion amongst the German people. Politics was in the air and on the streets. Out of sheer curiosity, Hitler would often participate in streetlevel political discussions with his drawing board and tee in his hands! His application for admission to the School of Arts and Architecture in Vienna – despite his sincere efforts and a strong desire to be an architect, was unfortunately rejected. His potential actually lay in a different field – politics. He was a gifted orator and he accidentally learnt that he possessed this skill – when he made a profound impact on people at a 'beer hall' (a place for discussing politics during those days).

> Adolf Hitler was asked to act as a proxy speaker for a senior political leader when Germany was going through political and economic turmoil after World War I. He addressed about 5,000 people in the above said 'beer hall' and he spoke with very little preparation, almost extempore. And he spoke for hours – stunning the audience with his logic, clarity of thought and oratory prowess. The audience consisted of seasoned German politicians of those days – and after his speech they acclaimed that if anybody could save Germany, it was Adolf Hitler. This is the power of potential.

Hitler had political acumen; he also knew the fine art of understanding world politics. In his book, Mein *Kampf*, he has reflected on the fact that for anyone who has to lead a nation, a deep political understanding at the grassroots, as well as the international level is required. In the political arena, he was known as the 'mad genius' – which he was. He rose to fall – but rise he did.

Another example that can be cited, is of Steven Spielberg, one of the few directors of Hollywood, who got a standing ovation at the Oscars. He loves making films. Time magazine has thrice dedicated its cover story to this mega director from Hollywood. He has earned fame worldwide, as well as a fortune doing what he always most wanted to do.

From his very childhood, he liked watching starry nights or a meteor shower. He was given a 8 mm camera by his parents as a gift when he was 12 years old, which opened a door to fantasy – the fantasy of films. He had made 15 short movies by the time that he was 16 years old! His passion for movies and the 'lights in the sky', took concrete shape when he made his first sci-fi movie, *Fire Light* with his 8 mm camera and a budget of $500 at that age. He had passion. Spielberg had talent and he recognised the fact that he was capable of doing great things even though he was young. He had faith in himself and his capabilities. He had potential. He started visiting Hollywood studios when he was 17 years of age. He used to hang around, trying to find out if someone would give him something to do. Nobody did. Nobody took him seriously because he was too young! After a lot of pleading and persuasion; he got into the production of a television series. He was hell-bent upon learning the art of movie-making from the nifty-gritties till the top, and he did! He made short films and TV serials. Some of them flopped and he had to wait a long, long time for a good break. Finally, in 1975, at the age of 28 he made Jaws. In Spielberg's words, it was an experiment with terror. It was a super-hit and broke all box-office records of movies like *The Exorcist, Gone with the Wind, The Sound of Music and even The Godfather.* It was a goldmine, to say the least. Making action movies that excited people, was the purpose of his life.

He gave us blockbusters like *Close Encounters of the Third Kind, ET, Raiders of the Lost Ark, Saving Private Ryan and Jurassic Park* to name a few. Very few know that he also made a couple of flops. This is when he made comedies like *1941*, which was a super flop by Hollywood standards. He quickly realised that comedy was not his forte – and that he should stick to what he knew best – action. He had learnt a fundamental principle from experience, the hard way, and we all must learn from this.

Spielberg's story tells us that we should follow our basic instinct of what we can do and what we can't. Once that is identified, go out to achieve your dreams with a sense of purpose. **Do only what you know best – identify your potential.**

His basic strength was passion and his potential. He had made it big by working for it and had stuck to it during difficult and trying times.

Walt Disney was a man who realised his dreams far beyond his wildest expectations. He loved what he did and chased what he loved – animated movies – and in return got 32 Oscars, five Emmies, five honorary doctorates and 900 citations. Besides all this, he was one of the richest men in the world.

From his childhood, he learnt that *small things can give you great joy*. Going for walks in the woods with his uncle and watching animals at play gave him great pleasure. These were the animals that he used throughout his career, to make the best animated cartoons in the world. He applied a simple principle that, 'To really succeed and be happy, you have to do what you enjoy.' Due to a poor harvest, the Disney family had to sell their farm and start a newspaper distribution business where the young Disney had to do back-breaking work from the age of 10 years. These tough times taught him an important lesson that there are people who succeed and those who don't. Throughout his difficult days, he had a burning desire to draw because he loved drawing. He also wanted to be a successful man – but on his own terms – doing what he liked.

He struggled to be accepted as a cartoonist with small advertising agencies. He got odd jobs here and there, but made the best of it by learning the ropes. He knew that he had originality and creativity, and used this to the hilt throughout his life. He had a difficult time entering Hollywood but never gave up. He started with the *Alice in Wonderland series* and later created *Mickey Mouse*, which quickly became an international celebrity – more popular than most Hollywood stars. He had immortalised a mouse, had made it a character and finally, an icon! He created his own school of art for cartoon animation. His school looked like a zoo, because it had live animals, that could be observed by the students. They could see the animals awake, asleep, eating, playing and so on. He created legends like *Snow White, Peter Pan* and *Cinderella*. He finally gave the world a new concept of entertainment – Disneyland.

He had followed two principles – doing what he liked best and believing in his ideas. A solid combination of passion and potential. **All great discoveries are made by men, chose feelings run ahead of their thinking.**

A stonecutter, who was not happy with himself, saw a merchant's house and wished that he became a rich merchant. God granted him his wish and made him a merchant. One day, he saw a king's minister coming to another merchant's house. He saw the fearful merchant go down on his knees in front of the minister. How powerful is the minister! 'God, I wish I was a minister', he thought and God made him a minister. As a minister he saw the power of scorching sun and wished that he was the sun. God made him the sun. He saw the clouds, stopping the sun rays – and God made him a cloud. The cloud was blown about by the wind and he thought the wind was the most powerful of all. Hence, God made him the wind. The wind could shatter houses, but couldn't move the rock. 'Oh God', thought the wind, I wish I could be a rock – the strongest of all', and God made him a rock. The towering rock looked down and saw a stonecutter cutting the rock!

The moral of the story is, be happy with the talent and resources that God has given you. You have your own specific strengths and these must be realised.

The Third P

Purpose: What does it mean to you?

A passion for something and having the potential and capability to pursue that passion is a fantastic combination – a wonderful potion. It is also important to realise how important all that is for you. There must be some sense of purpose in all that you want to do and all that you want to achieve. At a deeper level, you have to be convinced that whatever you are doing is right and that doing it, is important to you. It should be important enough for you, though it may not be so for others. Many times, it becomes a mission in life. Every passion-potential combination may not generate such a strong emotional feeling, which may culminate into the mission of a lifetime. Also it may not be necessary to have such strong feelings to be successful. But it is necessary for you to feel, what that means to you. Great actors say that acting has the effect of oxygen on them. Withdraw the opportunity to act, and they would die. Great leaders like Nelson Mandela have a strong sense of purpose. Mahatma Gandhi had a strong sense of purpose. Industrialists like JRD Tata had a purpose. **Purpose, in one sense, is believing in what you do and what you stand for. It gives you the courage of conviction.** Adolf Hitler had a very strong sense of purpose – to make his fatherland the most powerful nation in the world.

Once that you identify your passion-potential potion, start acting purposefully – and the rest will follow. Purpose also acts like an emotional goal at a higher mental plane.

*'It does not matter how slowly you go, so long as
you do not stop.'*

– Confucius

The Fourth P

**Perseverence: When the going gets tough, the tough
get going.**

Once you act out of conviction for a purpose, it gives
you strength to fight the odds. Many of us find our
passion-potential equation, but fail to act purposefully
and with vigour. People either don't act or give up too
soon. It is that die-hard attitude of a mountain goat, which
sees us through difficult times. It is here, that a strong
belief in yourself; your ideas and your purpose, help you
achieve that.

If

*'If you can meet with Triumph and Disaster
And treat those two impostors just the same
If you can bear to hear the truth you've spoken
Twisted by knaves to make a trap for fools,
Or watch the things you gave your life to, broken,
And stoop and build 'em up with worn-out tools
Yours is the Earth and everything that's in it,
And which is more – you'll be a Man, my son!'*

– Rudyard Kipling

Who is not familiar with Honda cars and bikes? It's a marvel created by a person who aspired to be the world's best mechanic! His role model was Napolean and his dream was to become the Napolean of mechanics.

Mr Honda was also short and frail like Napolean – 'if he could aspire to conquer the world, then why can't I,' he thought. A man should not be measured by his height – was the lesson learnt. He had a strong conviction that hard work and will power can take you to great heights. And he had a strong affinity for machines – a passion for them. He stayed away from his village and his parents for six years to learn his trade of repairing in a garage. He was innovative and at the age of 30 and got a patent for metal spokes for car wheels. He wanted to design better piston rings, but realised that he lacked technical knowledge. He, therefore, had the guts to enroll himself in a university of engineering at the age of 35. He would study at the university in the morning and work and apply what he had learnt in the evening at his workshop. He was thrown out of the university because he only attended classes dealing with the manufacture of automobile parts, skipping the rest of the curriculum. He wanted to learn and not merely earn a diploma.

'It does not matter what you are at school, it matters what you are at the school reunion.'

– Jamshed M Wadia

Honda had started his piston manufacturing factories with lot of dedication and hard work. These were destroyed in 1945, as a result of bombing by American. Japan had suffered a crushing defeat and its economy was in a mess. Honda realised that the Japanese now rode cycles because there was no public transport left and petrol was very expensive. Quick to react, he fixed a small motor to a bicycle – coming up with a cheap transport called the motorbike – which became an instant hit. He started a motorcycle assembly plant in February 1948 and set up the Honda motor company. His product was good, but he was in a financial mess. He knew that his strength lay in his technical acumen, what he lacked was the administrative ability – and he realised and accepted it. Through a friend, he hired Mr Takeo Fujisawa, an able administrator in his company, who turned the company around. Mr Honda would even say, 'If I had to manage my company on my own, I would have gone bankrupt because I am an inventor and not an administrator.' **So, stick to what you are good at, is the lesson learnt.**

Honda had a number of failures and setbacks, but he found an opportunity in every failure and went ahead where others would have given up – he believed, when the going gets tough the tough, get going. With all his financial problems and setbacks, he produced the fastest motorcycles in the world and proved to it that the Japanese could produce bikes as fast and reliable as anyone else in the world. This became his main purpose. In the year 1962, he entered the field of car manufacturing and was trying to take on the

US headlong! His cars entered the formula races and by 1965, his cars were beating other world famous brands, such as Ferrari and Lotus.

His story is a tale of perseverance, purpose and of course, passion. His is also a story of a dreamer – but of someone, who could dream hard and work hard. You can conquer the world if you have it in you, provided you are prepared to work hard with dogged determination.

If

'If you can make one heap of all your winnings
And risk it on one turn of pitch-and-toss,
And lose, and start again at your beginnings,
And never breathe a word about your loss:
If you can force your heart and nerve and sinew
To serve your turn long after they are gone,
And so hold on when there is nothing in you
Except the will, which says to them: "Hold on!"
Yours is the Earth and everything that's in it,
And – which is more – you'll be a Man, my son!

– Rudyard Kipling

Henry Ford is a perfect example of dogged determination to fight against the odds, an example of tenacity and belief in one's own ideas, and a passion for machines. His purpose in life, was to create a car for the people, which would run on petrol. The idea of building a machine that would travel the roads, obsessed him and almost haunted him till he really made one. Starting on his project at the age of 29, it took him 17 long years and countless sacrifices before he could achieve his goal! He worked in a factory in the morning and at his workshop at home, until late at night on his petrol engine. Genius is about possessing infinite patience, they say. His father wanted him to take up farming, the family profession, but Henry was cut out for machines. His father gave him up for lost, but America and the world found one of the greatest industrialists ever born. Many of us get ideas and also have the potential of carrying them out, but we are often scared of putting these ideas into action. While he was busy researching, he was offered a plum promotion but with a rider – stop working on petrol engines and work on electrical energy which the world at that time thought, would be the only source of power for the future. He was being asked to give up his dream in exchange for material security and a guaranteed future! A bird in hand is better than two in the bush, and most people would have jumped for such a secure job. **In many of us, the need for security is so great that we would be prepared to sacrifice our most ardent dreams. Henry Ford chose to chase his dream.**

His father tried to push him into farming, while his employers were persuading him to give up his dream for a promotion, the world was trying to tell him he was wrong. But he went ahead with his dream and made sure that it was a success in the end.

He also revolutionised the automobile industry by going in for mass production, using his unique idea of an assembly line, where the work was brought to the worker and not the other way round. What started out as a small dream, became an enterprise of sorts by 1970, employing 430,000 people with a wage fund of $3.5 billion!

He left behind a philosophical legacy by saying, 'Everything is possible, faith is the substance of things hoped for, the evidence of things not seen.' His statement is not at all by chance, it is backed by a life full of hard work – a man who had unshakeable faith in himself and the grit to fight all odds, ready to sacrifice for his dream.

If

'If you can keep your head when all about you
Are losing theirs and blaming it on you;
If you can trust yourself when all men doubt you,
But make allowance for their doubting too:
If you can wait and not be tired by waiting,
Or, being lied about, don't deal in lies,
Or being hated don't give way to hating,
And yet don't look too good, nor talk too wise
Yours is the Earth and everything that's in it,
And – which is more – you'll be a Man, my son!'

– Rudyard Kipling

The Litmus Test for Your Talisman

Having seen the basic four Ps for satisfaction and success, let us now look at finding out – what is my cup of tea?

How do I look for that Talisman which can become a beacon for me, to act diligently and purposefully? I have four questions for you. These four basic questions, if answered *honestly* can finally tell you what your cup of tea is, which will satisfy you and make you happy and successful. With these answers in place, you will be able to find your life partner – that activity – which will lead you to happiness and satisfaction. **I am laying so much stress on happiness and satisfaction because that is what success is. Let me assure you. Success measured by any other parameter that you have, will follow for pure.** So, read on.

• Is it a yearning?

What you like, attracts you. So if you feel that you like an activity – and if you actually like it – then this activity will always attract you. No matter what time of the day, no matter what the circumstances are, no matter what the weather is like – you are always for it. It acts like a magnet. People who like to talk to people – make great sales and marketing guys – because they always like to talk to people. Ruby Bhatia, the anchor-turned-actress just liked talking and she talked her way through many talk shows. Beckham would play football whenever he found an opportunity to. A guy who loves machines would always go to his backyard to repair an old engine even if it is the hottest of afternoons. Yearning is domain-independent and it could be the arts, science, technology or management. You love it, because you love it.

'People who are sensible about love are incapable of it.'

– Douglas Yates

• Does it satisfy you?

If this activity is your basic instinct – it must satisfy you. At a more basic level, do you get a kick out of it? A good cook loves cooking and standing in front of the hearth for eight hours, dishing out a wonderful meal gives him the greatest joy. A person who is into para-sailing, gets his greatest satisfaction when his feet are above the ground. A person who loves gardening is satisfied after he has worked in his garden for hours. While travelling in a bus from Dover to London, I happened to meet a hefty lady driver who was talking enthusiastically to all the passengers almost tirelessly. I was amazed at her enthusiasm and her dedication. I couldn't resist myself and asked her as to why she chose driving as a profession. Pat came the answer, 'Because I love driving.' To me, she looked absolutely satisfied. Remember, satisfaction is a state of mind.

• Is it easy to learn?

Your cup of tea must be easy to brew. If you love it, if it satisfies you – it must be easy to make. The activity, which you want to make a partner for life, must be an easy and comfortable one. Many people get into computer science and at a later date, regret it because, they don't have an aptitude for it. They find cracking all those logic-related problems very very difficult. They find the learning very painful. Drop this, if it happens to you. This is not your cup of tea.

• **Does it come effortlessly?**

Are you in absolute flow and ecstasy while having your cup of tea? AR Rehman, the great Indian music composer is always most excited and yet comfortable, while composing a piece of music. Zubin Mehta is in a state of ecstasy – as if possessed – when conducting the Philharmonic Orchestra. If you find your Talisman, it will be an effortless endeavour – an automatic flow – like a waterfall.

If the answer to the above four questions are in the affirmative – you bet you found your cup of tea – your Talisman which will give you satisfaction and eventual success. The answer to each one of these questions need not be a very strong 'YES'. As long as it is 'yes' and not a strong 'no', you have found your cup of tea – just go ahead.

Mr RK Laxman, the famous cartoonist who kept the Indian audience enthralled for more than five decades, is a simple man. He still prefers to drive in his black Ambassador car, not caring much for those sleek Mercedes, Skodas and Pajeros that most of us run after. Starting a career as a cartoonist with a daily in Mumbai, (then Bombay) he has risen to be the most admired and wittiest political cartoonist of India. His front-page cartoon in the *Times of India*, titled *You Said It*, always has an apt punchline and is a household name.

He has portrayed the whole genre of politicians, from Pandit Jawaharlal Nehru to Jagjivan Ram, Indira Gandhi and the entire political 'who is who' of India. He is the creator of the famous 'Common Man', who portrays an Indian very well. His passion for drawing can be seen in his work. Rolling out cartoons everyday for the front page of a national daily, requires a very agile mind and a firm grip on the political situation of the country. It also takes a very high degree of commitment.

One day, while I was with him, an acquaintance of Mr Laxman asked him if he could help evaluate the artistic work of a young budding artist, who wanted to be a cartoonist. Mr Laxman said that lots of people wanted to become artists, but most of them did not have the patience to learn and practice. Then he explained to me, how he sat down on roadside bus stands and travelled in trains in Mumbai for two full years, just in order to learn drawing creases and wrinkles on mens' shirts by watching them. This was a very small part of his entire learning process. How many of us who want to excel, have this type of determination? He knew that he could draw well and he loved it. He was prepared to work for it and wait for his turn to be noticed by the Indian masses. He had the passion, potential and the perseverance. His purpose was to keep the Indian masses informed about the feelings of a common man regarding Indian politics in particular and the Indian scenario in general. He is an example of a perfect connect between passion, potential, perseverance and purpose. He loves drawing cartoons and is very much at home with them – with his talisman, his 'cup of tea.'

IN A NUTSHELL

All those who love their jobs are never tired of work. Liking your work can be the single most important factor for success and satisfaction. Artists, players, scientists, engineers or men and women from any profession who get a kick out of their work have always done better in life, than those who work just because they have to work. It happens many times, that we discover our likes and dislikes much later in life. A number of people have changed their professions after working for even a decade – just to do something that they like. Money and earnings in such cases become by-products – but they definitely come. This kind of 'mid-course correction' may be a better idea than to keep steering towards the wrong direction throughout your life.

Talents and hobbies must never be overlooked. Basic talents, in fact, have become the reason for success of many great people. Therefore, identify your own talents and look for talent in others as well. Aligning your profession with your talent is a recipe for success. If you are not madly in love with your job, you can still make it enjoyable by being innovative and changing the job context and environment. Those who are in a position to change the environment for others, must make a sincere effort to do so – because this is the way one gets the best out of people.

The passion and potential to perform, a sense of purpose and perseverance, are the four basic ingredients for spectacular success. These are the four Ps of success. If you have these four Ps in you even to a little extent, you can be sure of success. Most importantly, one must align all these together to make things happen. Remember, making your cup of tea is the easiest. Your cup of tea attracts you, it satisfies you, it is easy to learn, and it is effortless to prepare. If any activity satisfies these parameters for you, then that's your cup of tea.

'When you go, go with all your heart.'
                                            – Confucius

Your Personal Road Map

1. List out your hobbies and talents.

2. What characteristics describe you best?

3. What is your passion and what are you doing to pursue it?

4. How can you change the context of your job to make it more interesting and exciting?

5. Identify your own strengths and map them onto the four Ps as discussed in the chapter.
   - Passion
   - Potential
   - Purpose
   - Perseverence

6

Being in Command of Your Feelings and Reactions:

Emotional Optimisation

'To go beyond is as wrong as to fall short.'

– Confucius

BEING IN CONTROL OF YOURSELF

To live well on a day-to-day basis, without being ruffled by what is happening around us would be a *vardaan* or a blessing that we all would ask for. The environment in which we live, work and socialise, has a telling affect on our behaviour and well-being many a times. So much gold and glitter, so many pulls and pressures, aims and aspirations often leave us with emotional scars – some of them lasting for long periods of time.

Can we live a balanced life where we act but do not react? Can we manage our personalities, so as to protect ourselves from emotional turbulences? Can we act and react appropriately for our own good? Yes, we can.

Vipassana, a technique of meditation, developed and practiced by Gautam Buddha 2,600 years ago, aims to achieve an eqanimous mind – which doesn't jump with joy when something very good happens to us and also doesn't get into a depression if something bad occurs. *Vipassana* shows one the way to *moksha,* or *mukti.* *Moksha* or *mukti,* imply liberation from all the negative feelings that we accumulate on our journey through life. The underlying philosophy of *Vipassana* is – 'observe, but don't react.' Observe and be aware of the minutest of feelings, but develop a habit so as, not to react to these feelings. This comes with practice and patience, but is not impossible to achieve. Most meditation techniques, directly or indirectly try to achieve this. **'Our happiness or being unhappy depends upon our reactions to our feelings.'**

In order for us not to react to a feeling, we should first feel the feeling and then try to heal it. It becomes important to be able to understand one's feelings and label each of them. Ask yourself, 'Is it anger that I am feeling now?' If you know that a situation is taking you towards anger or annoyance, you should be able to discern this before that anger gets hold of you. The realisation of the generation of the feeling, as it starts building up, is the first and most important step towards successfully controlling it and getting a hold on yourself. This is the training of your mind, which slowly becomes a reflex action.

Many a time, when we go through our mood swings, we don't make an effort to identify what is bothering us and what it is that we are feeling. Is it annoyance, anger or remorse? Once established, we can always go back in time to enquire whether it was a particular incident, person or situation, that brought about this feeling in us. What causes this feeling? Then, try and reconcile the situation so that we can quickly be rid of this negative feeling.

Remember, you have only one life to live – so you might as well live well, every minute of it, because every minute is precious and it belongs to you. If you lose it, you are the loser.

A popular curse in India is, '*Mein tumhe saat janam tak nahin bhooloonga*', which translated, means, 'I will not forgive or forget you for seven lifetimes.' This in fact, amounts to cursing your own self because you will be the one to sulk continuously and for so long. Why *saat janam* – even seven days of sulking is bad enough. Even a few hours of sulking is not worth anything. Imagine a situation, when someone comes and says something negative or unpleasant to you during lunchtime and you curse this person right upto dinnertime. Whose loss is it anyway? It is yours and not the person's who misbehaved with you. The longer you sulk, the happier he is. The earlier you get it out of your mind and your system, the better it is for you.

> A man was once seated at the breakfast table with his younger brother. The younger brother accidentally spilled some coffee on the table, which spoilt the older brother's shirt. He got up, gave him a tight slap and cursing and fuming, walked out without having his breakfast. He zoomed to the office on his motorbike and on the way, got a ticket from the cop for over-speeding. Eventually, he was late to office and got a mouthful from his boss. He spent a miserable day outside and came back home dead tired. Finally, he blamed his brother for the bad day. How wrong he was! Had he realised in the morning that it was only an accident and told his brother to be more careful in future, rather than cursing him, the problem wouldn't have been blown out of proportion. He could have gone to office as on any other normal day – probably earning more respect from his kid brother.

The moral of the story is that 10 per cent of whatever that happens to us, depends on outside factors and 90 per cent of things happen because of how we react to situations.

Develop a Philosophy for Happiness

We have to constantly invent and innovate to live a more meaningful and satisfying life. This is also a matter of attitude and viewing things differently. The best thing to do is not to let feelings that disturb us, get generated. A simple philosophy could help us live happily.

'The essence of philosophy is that a man should so live that his happiness shall depend as little as possible on external things.'

– Epictetus

We all are running fast, but the question is, where are we running? We often don't know what we want, but we do get carried away by what others do or have.

You normally feel that if everyone is running, they must be right, therefore, you start running too! This is the 'herd' mentality.

A five-bedroom house remains a house and doesn't become a home till there is peace and harmony among the people who occupy that house. We have started quantifying things so much that we have stopped enjoying the moment at hand – which will never come back. Such moments are so perishable that they can't be stocked like bank accounts. A 10-bedroom mansion is no guarantee for a good sleep.

'The paradox of our time in history is that . . . We have taller buildings, but shorter tempers; wider freeways, but narrower viewpoints; we spend more, but have less; we buy more, but enjoy it less. We have bigger houses and smaller families; more conveniences, but less time; we have more degrees, but less sense; more knowledge, but less judgement; more experts, but less solutions; more medicine, but less wellness. We have multiplied our possessions, but reduced our values. We talk too much, love too seldom, and hate too much. We've learnt how to

make a living, but not a life; we've added years to life, not life to years. We've been all the way to the moon and back, but have trouble crossing the street to meet the new neighbour. We've conquered outer space, but not inner space; we've split the atom, but not our prejudice. We have higher incomes, but lower morals; we've become long on quantity, but short on quality. These are the times of tall men, and short character; steep profits, and shallow relationships. These are the times of world peace, but domestic warfare; more leisure, but less fun; more kinds of food, but less nutrition. These are days of two incomes, but more divorce; of fancier houses, but broken homes. It is a time when there is much in the show window and nothing in the stock-room

Know Your Own Personality

On both sides of the spectrum of a balanced personality, there are two extreme types of people. The over-involved and the indifferent.

People who are over-involved, magnify their problems because they zoom into it. These people are disturbed by every little incident. Small problems for them, can be very upsetting and may unleash emotional storms. Those who concentrate too much on a disturbing event, magnify their own reaction, you can see such people clutching their seats very hard just before an aircraft is about to take off!

People who are indifferent, are hardly ever moved by any incident. They are thick-skinned and have the ability to 'switch off' or zoom out of an incident. Ideally, we should be in the centre of the 'emotional reactional spectrum.'

For those who are over-sensitive, it is advisable to avoid situations that can be disturbing and avoid job avenues that have a high degree of uncertainty or pressure, which they are unable to handle. Once you know your personality, you can also bring about a gradual change in your outlook so that you try to move towards a more balanced zone on the emotional spectrum. *Different people react differently to different situations.*

Adolf Hitler once said that if 100 problems were coming your way, 90 would get sorted out by themselves along the way. Only 10 problems are left in the end for you to actually handle. This approach has some sort of in-built practicality – especially for people who operate at higher levels of organisational hierarchies. Identify those major areas or problems that require your attention – delegate the rest.

Then there are men and women bereft of feelings. They are emotionally flat – unresponsive to any feelings. They neither feel, nor can they express their feelings. These are emotional 'duds.' They are failures as leaders, friends, peers, parents, subordinates as well as bosses. There are all sorts of people. Some are colour-blind, some don't know the colours, while others don't appreciate them.

Appropriate Emotional Response

'Wise men talk because they have something to say; fools, because they have to say something.'

– Plato

Displaying emotions is a manageable art. You cannot appear to be thick-skinned and have no feelings. Display of positive as well as negative emotional responses to situations is highly important for our relationship with people. The display of positive emotions can earn goodwill. It has a soothing effect on our colleagues, subordinates, friends and family. There are some people who greet you with enthusiasm and exuberance. They make you feel wanted and welcome. The catch is to 'make you feel.' Even if someone doesn't welcome you from the depths of his heart, but makes you feel wanted, the gesture will definitely make you feel good. Unfortunately, we do not pay adequate attention to this aspect and fail to greet or welcome people properly. I am not advocating a 'false front' approach, where you mask your feelings or misrepresent your feelings. I am referring to those people who want to welcome others, but fail to adequately demonstrate the fact. Even talking to someone on the phone after a good gap of time can be made peppy by emphasising on, 'Hi, how have you been?' at the start of the conversation. The idea is, not to seem *emotionally constipated,* when we actually are not so. Unfortunately, this is what happens frequently with most people – a lack of demonstrated enthusiasm.

An appropriate display of negative emotional responses like anger, displeasure, anxiety, criticism or rage are all equally important. In your capacity as a leader of a group, remember that you are its emotional guide. Overdoing things, or under-performing can demoralise the team, annoy someone or even jeopardise a relationship for good.

Over-sensitivity and lack of self-control both spell doom – they invoke responses disproportionate to situations. As a leader, therefore, one must appear in total control of oneself. People respect those who are calm and composed even in a crisis. Novelist, Ernest Hemingway has very aptly said, '**Courage is grace under pressure.**'

It is also important not to be sarcastic. Being sarcastic not only hurts the other person, it also shows you in poor light.

The art of Emotional Intelligence also lies in judging and realising the 'sensitivity level' of other people. Remember, all of us are not the same. Each one of us has an emotional threshold. While dealing with people on a day-to-day basis, it is important to realise and register their sensitivity levels and handle them accordingly. **Be very careful while handling sensitive people – you may inadvertently hurt them.**

Controlling Emotional Turbulence

'We cannot avoid birds from flying overhead but we can always stop them from making a nest in our hair.'

– A Chinese proverb

External Tripwire

We have no control on the point of time, when an emotion will be triggered. We also have little control on the form that the emotion would eventually take. This can be attributed simply to the fact that our emotions are generated as a response to a situation, and the reference point is external, over which we have no control. Each situation acts like a tripwire – invoking a reflex action from our side. There are simple common sense-based methods that can help us, once we hit the tripwire.

- *The Dwell Time*

We have little control on unforeseen situations or emotions for that matter, but we do have control to some extent on how long that emotion is going to last. This is what I would phrase as the dwell 'time.' Let that emotion – if it is a negative one not make a permanent home in your head. Shake it off as early as possible – and this can be managed. Because this is in your hands – You can at least, make a sincere effort towards it. If somebody says something unpleasant, you feel bad, but don't sulk and make your own life miserable. The art of handling yourself and living well is to reduce the 'dwell time' of negative emotions.

- *Use your rational mind to control your emotional mind*

Nature has given us human beings a rational mind; use it to control the emotional mind when you hit an external tripwire. When animals react to external inputs, they seldom know where to stop. That is why we use the expression 'barking like a dog' for someone who blabbers unendingly. If a door without a latch bangs whenever there is a breeze, a dog will bark every time that it bangs – no matter how many times it happens during the night. However, it would be different for us. We humans would examine the door once and on noticing that there is no latch, would make a mental note of the fact that there is no latch and thereafter, stop reaching out every time that the door bangs. The very next day, we would take action to get the door repaired. **Convincing yourself out of a situation or reconciling to a reality is the key to controlling emotional turbulence.**

'Let not the sun go down upon your wrath.'

– The Bible

- *The five-year test*

Most of us frequently make our problems look larger than life, or at least larger than what they actually are. This blows it out of proportion and obviously pushes us into an emotionally upsetting storm. When you introspect, you will realise that there have been situations that got the better of you and that you could label as 'disturbing' at that point of time. For example, not getting good grades in exams as you had expected, being overlooked for a salary raise which was your deserved due, missing a flight as a result of a traffic jam or a party because you were tied down with work. All these had upset you and snatched your happiness for a few hours or a few weeks. But most of these 'disturbing' events would look absolutely insignificant today. Those incidents that troubled you for days, have no meaning for you today. You may think 'Oh! How silly I was to have allowed myself to become upset over such trivial things.' What I am trying to say in a nutshell, is that problems, that upset us, are trivial most of the time and their significance melts away after a while. Why then, make them look big and get unduly upset with small issues?

So, whenever you face a problem or are confronted with an event, which could upset you emotionally, try to see and reason out, 'What will be its significance five years from now?' And let me assure you, in most cases you will find that the matter is absolutely trivial where there is no need to become unnerved and lose your sleep. This is what I call, 'the five years' test' and it works. **Time, therefore, is the greatest healing factor.**

- *Accepting the consequences*

There is another simple method of soothing yourself when you are in the middle of a difficult situation. This is a four-step method. Pick up a paper and pencil and write down the following.

- What exactly is the problem that is bugging me?

- What are its consequences?

- What is possibly the best way in which I can deal with this situation?

- I am prepared to accept the consequences of my actions/inactions.

The first three steps are questions and the fourth one is a resolve. **Most of the time our emotions go out of hand because of the fear of consequences.** The moment that you are prepared to accept the consequences, tension and negative emotions disappear. Half the battle is won. You can then, concentrate on how to solve the problem and what best actions to take in order to have total control over the situation. This is a very practical and a time-tested method, which works very well. Try it when you need it!

- *The Importance of Fun and Games*

Do let your hair down once in a while. Having fun is a good way of getting negative emotions off your mind.

It is important to develop a liking for games and hobbies. Do whatever that gives you a sense of relief, a feeling of well-being. This could be games, laughter, jokes, humour, parties, trekking, camping, reading books, TV, music or simply going for long walks. We must find time during the course of the day, to do things that please us.

In a nutshell, therefore, keeping our emotions in check is the key to our emotional well-being. This is also very important for our relations with people. If negative emotions dwell on us longer than the necessary period, they surely have a negative affect on us and also on the people around us.

Anger and Rage

'Anyone can become angry – that is easy. But to be angry with the right person, to the right degree, at the right time for the right purpose and in the right way is not easy.'

– Aristotle

When a car dangerously overtakes you, your reaction is 'That son of a —————' followed by more rage. You are so angry, that at times you feel like killing the guy – at least you say so. It's a fit of rage and you are on that 'hair trigger,' ready to yell at anyone without any provocation. You would also yell at the car, which honks from the rear. And you are snappy for a long, long time.

Of all our moods and emotions, anger and rage are the most difficult to control. Anger is self-energising and seductive. It can snowball and go out of control. Then, there are those who are cool and do not get angry easily. But there are plenty of people who are on a 'short fuse' – ready to fly off the handle, even with the slightest of provocation. If this goes unchecked, anger can be bad for health and it can be bad for our relationship with people. When you are angry, you don't know what you are saying – and often regret it later.

Many say anger cannot be controlled, some say it need not be controlled. Venting fury doesn't solve the problem. Catharsis, it has been proven beyond doubt, adds fuel to the fire. It doesn't douse the flames. Many feel that once they vent their anger on someone, they feel unburdened and good. First of all, it is wrong to think that you have done yourself good by spitting all the venom out. Secondly, even if it is right, what about the other person who you made the punching bag? He will surely not feel lighter for all your efforts!

'Anger is always a losing proposition.'

Why then, do we get angry?

People get angry when they are endangered – not always physically. You get angry if:–

- Your self-esteem is endangered.

- Your ego is hurt.
- Somebody insults you.
- You are deprived of something.
- Someone doesn't comply with what you want.
- Someone is doing something stupid.
- You are frustrated – you do not get what you want.

What can hence, be done to control anger?

Handling anger can be like handling the devil – you've got to be careful, patient and above all, innovative to be successful in nailing it down. These are a few things that can be done.

- **Challenge the thought which made you angry.** In this way, you can convince yourself that there is no good reason to get angry.

- **View things differently.** If someone zips past your car dangerously close, you could become furious or look at it differently. Viewing it differently could be a charitable thought as well. The poor fellow may be in a hurry to go to the airport or to a hospital. This will help you ignore the incident.

- **Accept the situation.** We often go against the current, which creates a problem. It rather helps, when one accepts the situation as it is. Remember, whenever we lose our temper, things don't go the way that we want them to.

- **Diffuse the situation.** We often find ourselves in a situation where there could be other people

involved. For instance, an argument in a meeting or in a coffee shop could take a nasty turn – and the situation could snowball. Use tact to avoid confrontations and make an effort to diffuse the situation. Remember, during a heated argument – everyone is irrational and arguments are never a
· solution to arguments.

'Those who fly into a rage, always make a bad landing.'

- **Don't vent your anger.** Even if you get annoyed, don't vent your anger on someone else. It will neither help you, nor will it help the other person.

- **Delay Action.** This, I think, is the most important aspect of anger management. We all fire from the hip and are trigger-happy. Sleeping over a problem or delaying taking action can sometimes be the biggest saving factor!

A regional marketing head once felt that his work was not being recognised by his seniors. The organisation, in fact, was going through a bad phase in business and all increments and promotions had been kept on hold. It was, however, not this person's fault. It was just that business was not doing well. One day, he got very upset and typed out a very nasty mail to his corporate marketing head. He read it twice to make sure the punch was a solid one – and pressed the return key. Moments after he had pressed the key, it dawned on him that he had made the wrong move – a very stupid move.

Sure enough, he lost his job within a month. In this case either he should have talked to his boss and sorted out the differences, or may be, saved the e-mail for a day or two, till he had cooled off and never ever sent the e-mail.

'In the midst of great joy, do not promise anyone anything. In the midst of great anger, do not answer anyone's letter.'

– A Chinese proverb

- *Coming back to the normal mood at the earliest*

Whatever solutions we may try to find, there are occasions when our temper gets the better of us. Somebody or something would still be able to annoy us and we would be likely to lose our temper. In such a situation, the best that one can do is damage control – for yourself and for others. Reduce the dwell time – the total amount of time for which you are angry *including* the sulk time, so that you minimise damage to yourself. As mentioned earlier, bring your mood back to normal in the shortest time possible. I also call it the 'NTP approach', bringing yourself to Normal Temperature and Pressure at the earliest. Don't spoil your day because of someone else – it is not worth it.

George Washington, the former president of the US, was a very short-tempered man. He tried his best to keep his temper in check, but still would blow his top occasionally. He was aware of this weakness and knew that it had serious inherent repercussions –

especially in a political work environment. He had, however, developed a knack for damage control for those who were at the receiving end of his anger. Once that he had cooled down after a flare-up, he would go to each person that he had a showdown with, and make all-out efforts to reconcile and patch up with them. This was his practical way to handling a situation and doing damage control. The moral of the story is, if you lose your temper, you must contain the damage done to the environment – the victims of your anger and also bring yourself back to the NTP to reduce harm to yourself. Studies now, point out that it takes merely six seconds for one's temper to get out of control, from the time that you are externally triggered (to which you lose your temper) and blow your top. It is, therefore, extremely important to be conscious and also cautious, whenever there is a build-up of anger within you. It has aptly been said, '**Anger is never without reason – but seldom a good one.**'

Handling Grief

Grief, again, is an emotional state triggered by external factors. The first thing to keep in mind, is that grief is universal. You are not the only one with whom things go wrong – it happens to everyone.

There was a young boy who died of snakebite. This was a huge shock to his mother who couldn't bear it. She started running from one doctor to another, visiting *hakims*, so that something could be done to revive her son. Since he was already dead, none could help her. Someone advised her to go to Lord Gautam Buddha, for help. She approached the Lord with folded hands and requested him to help her, and to bring her son back to life. Gautam Buddha realised her plight and understood the situation and her state of mind. He told her that he would be able to do something for her provided she got him a pinch of salt from someone's house and not from her own house. It appeared to be a simple task for her to get a pinch of salt from someone. The lady got up quickly and as she turned, Gautam Buddha called her back and told her, 'Please get this pinch of salt from a house where there has never been a death.' She went from house to house throughout the village, for that pinch of salt. She spent the whole day without success and returned only at night, explaining her failure and in the bargain, understanding that grief is universal.

'Nanak dukhia sab sansar.'

– Guru Granth Sahib

Guru Granth Sahib says, 'Grief is Universal.'

Handling grief is about handling yourself and handling people around you during that period.

During war, a battalion lost more than 300 soldiers in a single night operation. Losing more than half the battalion came as a big shock to the Commanding Officer and obviously, the entire battalion was grief – stricken. To lose those with whom you have spent more than half your life is not an easy task. It lowers the moral of the most courageous of people. Burying your kith and kin is a terrible task. This information was sent to the headquarters and pat came a very funny reply from the General. The message was that the General would be visiting the battalion the next day and would take a salute at a ceremonial parade! The Commanding Officer was shocked at the General's behaviour and his total lack of emotions and his understanding of the soldier's state of mind. Since it was an order and had to be obeyed, he mustered up the survivors and informed them about the ceremonial parade the next day. They had to prepare their uniforms, shine their boots and belts, polish all the brass – while there were 300 dead bodies on their hands! There was no choice, the order was to just do it.

The very next day, the General arrived. He cancelled the parade, but instead, addressed the men. This is what he said, 'You all must have thought that I am a heartless fool who, under such trying circumstances wanted to see a ceremonial parade. You all must have been cursing me for the last 24 hours – and that is what I wanted you to do while you buried your dear ones. Cursing me would have reduced your emotional trauma – and that is what I wanted to do to help you.

The moral of the story is that there can be innovative ways of doing things. At the same time, when you look around, you see that there are people who have problems, much worse than yours.

Whenever I travel through parts of the country where people live in slums, I always thank God for giving me a decent standard of living.

There is no single formula to handle grief, but one must remember that grief is universal, and everybody has to face it.

Emotional Hijack

'Courage is resistance to fear, mastery of fear – not absence of fear.'

– Mark Twain

Our emotional brain had developed much earlier, than our rational brain had. As the human race evolved, our emotional responses were developed to suit our survival. Fear and anger were given to us by nature to handle and deal with life-threatening situations. That is also the reason why our emotional mind works almost 80,000 times faster than the rational mind. It is designed to react in emergencies – which the rational mind is not equipped to handle. Sometimes, this gift of the nature can backfire and situations get out of hand. This defence mechanism, given to us, is etched into our nervous system – inherited by us through millions of years of our evolution, through our ancestors.

There was once a petty thief who had a loving daughter. His daughter wanted him to lead an honest life and could convince him to reform himself. As luck would have it, his daughter fell sick and needed a surgery for her cure. The old man who had given up stealing, now decided to go for it for the last time and pick up money, just enough for her surgery. He started keeping an eye on a house where two working women lived. They would leave in the morning and return late in the evening. Taking it as a soft target, he entered the house one day, well past the time for the girls to go to work. Unfortunately, he was confronted by one of the girls who had taken ill and had decided to stay home. He tied her up and gagged her too. As he was picking up some stuff from the house, the other girl returned from the bus stop to pick up her umbrella, which she had forgotten to carry. He overpowered her and tied her up too! The girl said that she would feel suffocated if he gagged her and pleaded with the thief not to gag her – promising him not to make a noise or raise an alarm. This old man tells them that he would not harm them as he was only interested in picking up a few things from the house. He quickly collects all that he wants and as he is about to leave, the girl whose mouth was not gagged – yelled that she would report the matter to the police and would make sure he went to jail. This threat hit him like a sledge hammer and he clearly saw himself behind bars, as his daughter struggled with her disease without medical treatment.

Rage built up within him, he picked up a bottle of wine from the table nearby and smashed it on her head – killing her on the spot. Seeing the horror-struck expression on the other girl's face, he picked up another bottle and killed her as well. A petty thief, whose intention was to only pick up a few things from a house, became a murderer – killing two people in less than three minutes! This is 'emotional hijack', when the emotions can get the better of you.

There are a number of cases in which emotions get hold of people before they can get a hold on their emotions. There are movies that depict such incidents – when a blackmailer pushes a victim beyond a point and forces him to take harsh action – many times killing the blackmailer in turn.

A practical point of views in regard to these incidents could bring home a lesson or two.

The first, lesson is that, never push a person to the wall – never try to corner or trap a person. Remember, if you corner even a small rat, he will retaliate and fight back in desperation.

The **second lesson** to be learnt is, never let the water cross the 'brink.' The moment that water is allowed to cross the brink, in any situation, it goes out of control and that is the point of no return – leading to a crisis. This technique is called 'Brinkmanship'! Keep this always in your mind when confronted with a tricky situation.

The third lesson is, while dealing with people and situations, always provide them with an 'escape route'. Never trap someone. Let him save his face. Allow a person to get out of the situation gracefully. This is a very important aspect of interpersonal relationship at home, in the workplace as well as social circuits.

Even at diplomatic levels amongst nations, 'Brinkmanship' is employed very effectively. The pressure is always built up in 'notches' to have your way – never allowing the situation to go out of hand. Escalation and de-escalation of tension is a mastered art even amongst nations. Remember, war is the last resort when everything else fails. Many wars have been prevented with good diplomacy and tact – why then, can't we handle situations with tact?

We can!

Peer Pressure is no pressure!

> *'Nobody can make you feel inferior. Without your consent.'*

The so-called peer pressure works at all ages and at all stages of life.

Peer pressure is the pressure generated by a class of people whom we consider to be our equals. In that 'class of people' we always want to be either 'seen' as the best or at least be accepted as an equal.

There are many people who let peer pressure work positively for them. For example, in a school where there are boys who work hard to get more marks than their classmates. Some of them would play hard and vow to pick up the Best sportsman award.

However, there are people who let peer pressure work negatively on them. They don't make an effort to outshine others and are also unable to correctly assess their overall potential, ending up with a huge complex. **OK – if you**

are not good at maths, can you outshine others in football? If you are not a good cricketer, can you beat others in a debate and prove your point? Yes you can, remember that there are two or three things, that you can perform better than 50,000 other people, and this secret is known only to you.

> Honda was a short-statured boy who could not make it as a good sports person at school. He bounced back and used his mental abilities at academics to outshine not only his schoolmates, but also to bring honour and fame to his country.

Then, there are others who try to outsmart everyone through materialistic extravagances. This habit starts in schools with dad's money, when you own the most expensive pen or the latest bike – with very little of your own efforts. If it is your own self-esteem that you are trying to bolster, then God damn it **let it be through your own efforts! Not your dad's.**

There was once a boy, who studied in college. Coming from a family of meagre resources, he didn't have a two-wheeler. Everybody else in his class had swanky bikes. He was a cheerful guy who was good at his studies and his extra-curricular activities. He would participate in all activities of the college and would walk up to the venue whenever required. His friends were always willing to give him a lift on their bikes, but he never took their obligation and walked his way through. So much so, that he made walking a fashion statement! He would always be the last one to reach the cafeteria – but people waited for him and respected him for what he stood for. He never felt inferior – in fact, he made his situation very positive.

These qualities are to be learnt early in life and people who live beyond their means, are big 'show-offs' who can never get rid of the habit. Here starts the rat race. Looking at others and what they have, often blurs your own vision. You don't realise what exactly you want and most importantly, what you *should* want. Since you want to beat others at it, you put yourself in an *overdrive.*

As people go through their colleges, and settle down into jobs, they get married. To a large extent wives are great contributors in this overdrive. Remember, behind every successful man, there is a woman. And when both husband and wife are working, they drive each other crazy. Now, there are two rats competing with one another and the rest of the world! Today, even kids can put their dads into an overdrive by telling them that they have a smaller car than Mr so-and-so!

This is, in fact, the reason for the societal erosion that we witness today. We are not contented with what we have, often setting up 'false targets' for ourselves, overdriving ourselves – and often driving ourselves crazy.

Parents, wives, husbands and children, all of them are to collectively take the blame for pushing one another into the rat race and generating tension, often putting the blame on 'peer pressure.' At the same time, each person should individually be able to resist that temptation – whatever it is, to ward off the pressure.

In a nutshell, one should work hard to achieve realistic personal targets, aims and aspirations – but not as a result of pulls and pressures created by others.

Power and Adaptability of the Human Mind

We have a stronger will power than we think we do. Unfortunately, most of us have never had an opportunity to comprehend how much will power we actually possess.

In the armed forces, special training is imparted for survival under extreme conditions. The commando training course of the Indian Army and the US Marines are famous for stretching people to their extreme physical capacities. One has to go through battle obstacle courses that often stretch upto 2 km at one go. These training sessions also put one through speed marches with more than 20 kg of weight on one's back. Every week, the pressure increases, the first speed march being 16 km – which is 10 miles flat. The next three weeks take one through 26 km, 32 km and 40 km of non-stop jogging with a backpack of 20 kg! This requires one to be in an absolutely fit physical condition. More than physical, it is mental tenancity, which takes one through these extreme tests. The last few kilometers especially, is more of a test of one's will power than physical fitness. I have seen people cry with pain, but not give up on the last 1 km, only on the strength of their sheer will power. There are banners all over, with the motto – 'When the going gets tough, the tough get going.' I have seen very frail-looking guys make it, while big, tough-looking guys give up – guys, who lack that will to push themselves forward.

There is also a 'confidence jump,' where one is expected to climb a tower and crawl along a rope at 100 feet, come to the centre and let go to fall free into a pool down below. It is almost three times the 10 meter board and is difficult to perform. It is called the 'confidence jump' because it builds up confidence in a person. It is a mental benchmarking for the future that gives you tremendous confidence when you are in actual battle.

Any long-distance or marathon runner would agree that the last mile is all a game of sheer will power. Your knees give up but your heart doesn't.

The human body and especially the human mind are very adaptable. Will power is linked to self-denial, perseverance and delayed gratification. When one is developed, the others get alleviated automatically. Most religions of the world preach fasting. There is more to fasting than merely giving your system rest.

Regular fasting not only cleans your system, it more importantly, also gives you that inner strength through self-denial.

A day-long fast means, you don't eat while others do. It is a ritual, which teaches one discipline and brings in regimentation.

People with a strong will power become achievers through sheer perseverance.

The story of Ray Kroc is a story of dogged determination and perseverance – the man who saw potential in making quality hamburgers and feeding the world. He tried his hand at real estate, at selling paper cups and milkshake mixers with no great success. He then got into business with the McDonald brothers as their partner, selling hamburgers through a chain of McDonald restaurants. His is a story of determination to succeed, backed with attention to detail and the quality of product and service. In 1961, at the age of 52, he bought the chain's operations from the McDonald brothers for 2.7 million dollars – a large sum then and a large sum now. His meteoric rise in fact, started after the age of 52. He financed this sum through bankers and financers. His *mantra* was quality, service, cleanliness and value. He fanatically worked towards the consistency of service and quality of product to achieve a $3 billion annual sales of burgers by the year 1985. He suffered from diabeties and arthritis, but despite his agonising physical pain, he worked his way through making McDonalds an international name – second to none. He worked till the end of his life, spending all his time towards expanding his business. By the year 2003, McDonalds had more than 30,000 outlets with an annual sale of $ 40 billion!

Jealousy and Creative Frustration

Jealousy is a common ailment and manifests itself as a strong emotion amongst people. When I am jealous I say, 'Why does he have something that I don't? And obviously I pray that the other person should be denied what I don't have. Jealousy is obviously, destructive. When I am envious I say, 'I wish I had what he has'. Jealousy does no good because it imparts a negative, frustrating feeling and also shows one in poor light. The genesis of jealousy lies in insecurity, or when one is not happy with what one has.

Jealousy is not the manifestation of a single emotion – it is a bundle of different emotions. It can manifest itself in anger, hurt, anxiety, agitation, sadness, low self-esteem or even hurt and frustration.

In case that we transform jealousy and the ensuing frustration into solid action, it becomes what can be termed 'creative frustration.' All high achievers are envious of other successful people, but can utilise their emotions to pitch in with enthusiasm and become winners. They use their frustrations as a creative energy.

A prime example of someone with perseverance, a die-hard attitude and real creative frustration, is Thomas Watson – one of the founders of IBM.

He started his career as a small-time sewing machine salesman, learnt the ropes of the business from whoever he could, had the guts and craving for success. He opened a butcher's shop and had to close down his business when his partner cheated him. He was penniless but knew what he was good at – selling.

He joined a company called National Cash Register (NCR) and did well for himself. Some legal problems, however, landed the company in trouble and Watson had to leave. He swore to himself that he had to build a bigger business than NCR. He was frustrated, but used this to bring about a radical change and a turning point in his career. He was going to be the founder of the world's most prestigious brand – International Business Machines – better known as IBM. He was envious of NCR and wanted to make something bigger than that. He wanted to beat the NCR. He knew his strengths in marketing and had infinite faith in his experience. He was also a great motivator and could often touch the emotional chord of the organisation through his talks and coining great slogans.

He knew the worth and importance of manpower, sometime as early as the beginning of the twentieth century. By the year 1980, IBM had 340,000 employees and a revenue of $ 24 billion. He achieved this with his determination to fight competition. His advise, as can be read from his autobiography is, 'Nothing in this world can take the place of persistence. Talent will not: nothing is more common than unsuccessful men with talent. Genius will not: unrewarded genius is almost a proverb. Education will not: the world is full of educated derelicts. Persistence and determination alone are omnipotent.'

His is also a story of going that extra mile. He always worked harder than what he was paid for. In the end it paid of.

IN A NUTSHELL

In order to be happy, satisfied and successful, one has to be in control of one's emotions. You should be able to identify your feelings and see them build up so that you can control them. You must also analyse your own personality to see if you are insensitive or over-sensitive. It is important to display both your negative and positive emotions appropriately and try to judge people's individual sensitivity levels to deal with them accordingly.

Whenever you land up in a tight situation, remember that you have hit upon a tripwire. Use your logic to convince yourself to get out of the situation. Reduce the amount of time that negative emotions stay in your system – sulk for the least amount of time!

Losing one's temper is always a losing proposition. If you make concerted efforts, you can succeed in controlling this devil – it is difficult – but with practice and awareness – not impossible. During a setback, look at others. Grief is universal, but you are not the only one who is grief-stricken. Don't feel inferior because it is a complex that you have created for yourself and not your peers, so don't ever feel inferior.

Let me assure you, you have a stronger will power than you think you do – put it to test once in a while – be innovative.

Be jealous of those who are doing better than you, but don't sit and sulk – do something about it. Perform better than them and use this frustration as a creative frustration and you will succeed, be happy and be happy for others.

> *'It is better to keep your mouth shut and let people think you are a fool than to open it and remove all doubt.'*
>
> – Mark Twain

Your Personal Road   Map

1. Seeing the present day environment of the materialistic world, is it possible to keep your ambition under check? Discuss/write.

2. Our happiness or being unhappy, depends upon our reactions to our feelings.   Discuss/write.

3. You have lost your temper and created a scene. What damage control measures can you undertake?

4. Write about an incident where you acted courageously (courage need not always be physical, it could be moral or ethical).

5. If you are in a bad mood, what efforts can you make to change it and become cheerful?

6. From now onwards, promise to demonstrate your positive feelings through an appropriate emotional response.

7. While dealing with people at home as well as at work, make a deliberate effort to assess the 'sensitivity level' of people.

8. Make it a habit to come back to your normal mood after every outburst/impulsive response.

9. What steps will you take to bolster your confidence and self-esteem so that you do not succumb to peer pressure?

10. Were you ever 'overpowered' by emotions and acted irrationally to regret later? Please elaborate.

7

Social Competence and Leadership:

Applied Emotional Intelligence

'The most difficult gadget to operate is a human being. It has invisible buttons, but if you press the right ones, it works!'

NEED FOR SOCIAL COMPETENCE

'We have different ideas and different work, but when you come right down to it; there is just one thing we have to deal with throughout the whole organisation – that is the man.'

– Thomas Watson, founder IBM

These are golden words from a person who started IBM, and were spoken somewhere in the beginning of the last century. They are still so very true and would remain so for all times to come.

We have to deal with each other not only at work, but also at home and all other places of social interaction. However professional we may be, whatever salary we may bring home or whichever status we may enjoy in society, we would never be able to make a mark and be successful unless we know how to handle people around us.

All of us have strong individual personalities and we are all independent entities with our own convictions and beliefs. But we all have to work in teams at home as well as at work. There is a need to get along with other team members so that we are accepted as a worthwhile member who can contribute effectively. It is also important to be competent, which allows us to extract and commit maximum contribution from other members of the team.

With the advent of communication technology, we are always in touch with the people with whom we deal. It is, however, important that your touch be soothing each time that interaction takes place. The best of professionals and intellectuals have messed up their lives at home as well as at work, just because they didn't know how to deal with other fellow human beings. **You should be able to handle a man without manhandling him.**

Today, interpersonal skills – a new, fancy name for dealing with people – has become a mandatory requirement in order to fit into any job.

The Art of Relationship Management

'We learn from experience that men never learn anything from experience.'

– Bernard Shaw

The art of dealing with people does not start and end at plain smiling or being a goody-goody person. It goes beyond superficial behaviour, to a role where you can exercise some sort of an 'Emotional influence' on others. To reach somewhere close to this, you must have that 'emotional sensitivity' so that you can feel and understand how someone else is feeling. Your emotional antenna is always picking up signals whether you are sitting and chatting in a cafeteria with your friends, talking to the cop who is handing you a ticket for over-speeding, or discussing a serious financial deal in a board room. All those who tune into these signals and listen carefully can feel and assess situations from the other person's perspective.

'Tact is the art of making a point without making an enemy.'

– Howard Newton

You also require self-control to keep your own emotions in check so that you can tune into the other persons' requirements. Many times, most of us are so overwhelmed or swamped by our own emotions in a situation, that we fail to connect with what others are saying and more importantly, what they mean. The third ability is to act in a way that would influence and re-shape others emotions. Therefore, social attunement (to feel how others feel), self-control and the ability to influence others emotionally are three basic ingredients of the art of managing people.

Managing emotions in others, is in fact at the centre of the art of relationship management. This ability allows you to handle and shape situations, manage difficult people, win an argument, crack a business deal or make an affective speech to influence and motivate others, and soothe and calm down agitated people. It is the art to master people and situations.

At the higher end of the spectrum, these are the very qualities that diplomats, politicians, corporate leaders and good managers possess.

Once, Emperor Akbar had a dream that he had lost all his teeth. He called in an experienced astrologer to interpret his dream. The astrologer said, 'The dream means that all of your majesty's relatives will die before you', Akbar was very upset and sent the astrologer to jail.

A few days later, Akbar asked Birbal, his favourite and most witty minister to interpret the dream and Birbal said, 'The Emperor would live a longer, healthier and more fulfilled life than any of his relatives.'

Birbal got a huge reward for his interpretation.

The moral of the story is, it is important to know how to put your point across.

How People Influence People

Influencing people at the emotional level can produce results, that can be nothing short of spectacular. Most people are influenced by money, but money motivates only to a certain extent and only for a while. In one of my discussions with a group of people, there was a clear mandate in favour of money being a great motivator. We were on the sixth floor and I asked them as to who would volunteer to jump out of the window for 6 lakh rupees. Obviously, no one did. I then raised the stake to 10 lakh rupees for the tenth floor and it still didn't work! I am merely trying to bring home the fact that money can buy time and effort, but not sacrifice and loyalty.

- *Faith and belief*

  The prime mover that motivates people to make a sacrifice and go beyond the call of duty is faith or belief. From the religious point of view too, it is faith, which can give you strength in a crisis. Looking back on history, we know that people have fought wars and died to protect their faith.

When people worship an idol, which could be a piece of wood, stone or clay, they do not regard it merely as a piece of stone. *'Na Mano to Patthar, Mano to Bhagwan'* **which means, 'If your are faithless, it is a piece of stone, if you have faith, it is God himself.'** Generating faith on a human level is equally effective. Adolf Hitler awakened Germany and made the Germans believe that they were the best – second to none and that they could defeat the whole world. Materialistically speaking, Germany had very little after the First World War, but they were shown hope, had faith in their leader and started believing in themselves. This is what the highest level of leadership and motivation is all about. It inspires confidence in people.

'Faith is one of those words that connotes, however irrationally, some kind of virtue in itself.'

– Loius J Halle

A soldier fights for his country's and his own honour. He fights for a cause and can make the supreme sacrifice. He *believes* that he is fighting for a cause. The pay, which he gets at the end of the month, hardly compensates for the sacrifice of his life and limb.

A freedom fighter also fights for a cause – a slogan or/ and a belief. He is prepared to go to prison for decades. He is prepared to die, even as a human bomb. His is a cause, that is motivated from the heart.

'Sarfaroshi ki tamanna ab hamare dil mein hai.'

– Bhagat Singh

A mercenary fights for money, not a cause. He is never prepared to lose his life – because he wants to come back, spend the money and have fun. His faith and creed is MONEY.

If organisations can generate faith in people, which in turn means positive, unconditional trust in the organisation, then people can perform fantastic feats. Faith is also value-based and cause-based – it is a value system, that has a cause worth fighting for.

If a leader can generate faith to the extent that people trust him and believe everything that he says – he can expect loyalty at a far deeper level.

During survival courses that the armed forces conduct, a common exercise is 'The Great Escape', where five people have to make their way out of the middle of a jungle, without a compass or a map, at the dead of night. This group has to collectively find a way out and reach home – all of a 20 km-long trek. There is tremendous pressure on everyone and everybody desperately seeks to find the shortest and the surest way out. In such a situation, a person who can assure the group that he would be able to find a sure way out, emerges as the leader. In this kind of a situation, only faith works – faith in the leader.

- *Philosophy*

Philosophies have influenced people on the emotional plane throughout recorded history. Philosophies are also a set of rules and beliefs, that are convincing at their very core. There have been great influencers like Karl Marx, who influenced the way nations and people of nations think. The genesis of social and political movements have been on the basis of philosophies. This in turn, has created many nations. There have been the likes of Acharya Rajnish, who with their philosophy could bring serenity and a sense of well-being to millions. Men and women, have looked up to such people and placed them on a pedestal, attributing to them, qualities of godliness, almost equating them to God! Organisational cultures and philosophies can often find a congruence with one another.

- *The gift of the gab*

'Ask what you can do for the country and not what your country can do for you.'

– John F Kennedy

Words spoken at the right time, on the right occasion in front of the right people by the right kind of person can have a profound impact. What John F Kennedy said about four decades ago, urging Americans to move forward, has become a historical statement of sorts, often repeated by many leaders even today.

Eloquent speakers with their oratory skills have been able to move crowds to a frenzy. 'Masters of the mouth' have changed even the course of history. There have been very few speakers of the calibre of Adolf Hitler, who could speak non-stop for hours together and keep the crowds mesmerised, even making them go hysterical. It was the pure magic of his oratory skills – punch lines, and voice modulation that did the trick. When a reporter from the BBC tried to analyse the Fuhrer's speeches, he was shocked to find that in one long, resounding speech of six hours' duration, he spoke actually only on four issues!

It is not what you speak – sometimes, it is important how you speak. What you speak about, shows your logical skills and how you speak shows your emotional skills.

There have been legends like Winston Churchill and Fidel Castro who could keep their countries afloat during the worst periods of crisis, by managing to speak to the people of their country in a manner that mattered. To top it, this was 'plainspeak' because there were no electronic facilities to back it up. Those days, there weren't too many acoustics and no television. Plain microphones and radio was all that was available! Public speaking at this level is connected to charisma. Pandit Jawaharlal Nehru could hold his fellow-parliamentarians listenting in rapt attention and the Indian masses glued to their radios when it was needed.

Today, we talk of corporate communications and depend beyond moderation on computer-based power-point presentations. **Unfortunately, if you are not able to touch that human chord, there is neither any power nor any point.** People must rely less and less on the skills of computers and should fall back to their own skills of plainspeak. I call it 'crutchless talk'. Practice as much as you can, rehearse as much as required, but do speak well – it matters.

> *'If you haven't struck oil in your first three minutes, stop boring!'*
>
> – George Jessel

• Power of the Pen

The pen is mightier than the sword – in today's world, it is even mightier than an atomic bomb. This is no exaggeration, because philosophies, ideas and prophesies have reached varied audiences through books, journals, magazines and newspapers. Authors like Ayn Rynd, Jeffrey Archer and Fredrick Forsyth have portrayed characters, that became larger than life.

When you read a book and then see a movie made on the same story, it is often observed that the book was more captivating than the movie. The reason is simple. On celluloid, it is the director's perspective that is projected, which has to be a 'singular view.' When *you* read a book, you can view it and interpret it the way you want to. It is limited only by your imagination and emotions. That is the reason why written communication skills are very important. And as you go up higher in the hierarchy of the organisation, you are expected to convey much more in the least amount of words!

The power of the written word should never be underestimated. Many business proposals and political mandates have bombed because they were not rightly worded.

- *A central theme which appeals*

Examine movies which have been successful at the box office. A strong story line and a strong central theme are a must. Good performance by actors, photography, action and overall presentation come in later. It has to be based on a theme that appeals to the heart. It is a central theme that people can understand and relate to. The director also has to understand the emotions of the audience – what do people connect to? Whether it was *Saving Private Ryan* by Steven Spielberg or *Lagaan* by Ashutosh Gowarikar – both the movies had a strong central theme. That, is the reel world. In the real world too, there is the need to go along with a central theme while communicating with people. Your ideas must crystallise into a central theme, which can then become the focus of presenting a case. Good speakers normally select a theme and then look for a few connected issues and build their argument.

Make this a habit – at least be conscious of it to start with – it then becomes very simple to put your point across. I have tried to put across a few major areas that influence people. Now, I would briefly discuss human desires, that motivate people from their innermost being. Let us also see how you can touch people's hearts – the crux of social competence.

Motivation, Emotions and that Extra Mile

Enthusiasm, excitement, 'zing' and motivation are all closely linked. Excitement, desire and enthusiasm are in fact, the emotions that motivate us. After a defeat or a failure, negative emotions that make a person feel tired, exhausted and often demotivated are generated. A good achievement or a good result, gives you that pep, that additional energy to perform your best.

Positive emotions energise people to be active, productive and generate that 'want' to do things. This also generates creative behaviour to do something different and to go beyond and achieve extra. If one can generate positive emotions in people, then one can expect them to walk that 'Extra mile.'

Achievement and the desire to achieve are the basics of motivation. Great actors are motivated to give fifty takes because they desire to give their best shot. Cricketers and golfers practice everyday because they desire to do well. **If high performance is to be sustained, motivation must come from the inside out rather than outside in.**

Desire is actually the key to motivation, which is the source of sustainable motivation because it works on the emotional plane. Slogans like, 'We believe in the best', 'Customer care is our motto' and 'Be the best', are all motivators at the emotional plane, trying to ignite that desire within us, to be the best. There are 10 major wants and desires, that motivate human beings. If you allow these wants to be fulfilled, people get charged with energy. If you block these wants, people work like zombies and robots – doing what they are told to – not moving an inch more!

Basic Wants and Desires that Motivate Humans

- *Ownership*

We, as humans, are all possessive. Even a small child doesn't let his toy go. If someone tries to snatch his toy, he fights for it. The attitude of 'this is mine', is important. It could be a car, a house or any other commodity. At a presentation or discussion, if someone 'steals' your original idea, you feel extremely hurt. People are as possessive about their ideas and their original thinking, as any other worldly material.

If ideas are blocked, rejected or overlooked, people get hurt, dejected and demotivated. I hear this very often from people whose ideas have been sidelined, 'The next time I will not give any ideas in a meeting.' It has happened to many of us. At the workplace, it is important to hear out people and make everyone feel wanted, important and tell them that their ideas are important for the organisation or a common cause. Let people have a feeling of ownership.

When you say, 'it is your show, run it', believe me it works wonders. I have seen groups of executives or even groups of students work day and night to ensure that everything runs smoothly when given independent charge of a seminar, because they feel 'it is my baby.'

Inter-house competition in schools, inter-college competitions and inter-departmental healthy competitions in organisations, are all methods of making people feel that it is their show. Also remember, when you give charge to someone, let him have the feeling of ownership – he will never let you down. **He has to let himself down first, before he can let you down!**

- *Power, Independence and Autonomy*

Every human being wants to be in control of things. But every organisation wants to be in control of people. What a dichotomy! Freedom. Freedom to make a choice, freedom to outline and schedule your work, freedom to work in your own exclusive style are the basic desires that most of us nurse.

There are too many constraints on people, when they should come in, when they should go and what they should wear. In fact, there are also too many measurements in terms of output. We have started evaluating people like amplifiers, that this amount of input should give that quantity of output. Sure enough, they have started behaving like machines, they too, give not an ounce more and not an ounce less!

As long as you define the basic ground rules and the basic framework, people should be empowered to take their own decisions. Old economy organisations, as well as old economy leaders were fond of too many feedbacks, too many checks and balances and too many procedures. In the new economy, people call these 'systems' – is this a case of old wine in a new bottle? You must have systems, but systems should not be over-bearing and should allow enough breathing space and flexibility. Even a leader or a manager must provide autonomy at all levels. When you tell a guy that I want this to be done – do it the way you want to. This will generate enormous creativity and initiative. A reasonable measure of autonomy with reasonable feedback mechanisms can give a boost to your interpersonal skills. Autonomy let me tell you, empowers people to perform wonders. In fact, autonomy, power and ownership all go hand-in-hand. Remember, if you create conformists, you are sure to kill creativity. Dr Mujumdar, founder-Director of Symbiosis, provides full autonomy to all institutes. When you ask about the best way to handle people, he quips, 'The best way to handle people is not to handle them!' Having faith in your team and delegation of responsibility is a very strong leadership trait that pays in the long run.

- *Association*

A survey shows that given an option to work from home, only less than 10 per cent people would like to do so. We need company, we need people to talk to. People have a strong desire to associate with others – a sense of belonging to a team. There is always a peer-to-peer support and a boss-to-subordinate support. Organisations, in fact provide the space for quality social interaction. Many of us have a friends' circle at our place of work. People want to come to work because they like meeting other people. Then why say, 'Thank God it is Friday?' And why have Monday morning blues? These things happen because they do not want to meet bad people in bad organisations! The key, therefore, to motivate people is to provide a healthy, friendly atmosphere to which people are attracted, where they come in and are appreciative of one another. The desire to associate can be leveraged in order to make people work for more than the stipulated time – and also get quality work from them.

- *Excellence and Competence*

You are confident, when you are competent. Once you are confident, you have a sense of pride and self-worth, which leads to high self-esteem. We all have a natural gift to learn. We all want to be competent in our jobs and those who excel in their jobs have a higher motivational drive.

To know your job well is a great feeling, which gives a lot of satisfaction. In order to motivate people, one has to act like a coach, making people feel and realise that you want them to be good at their jobs – competent and excellent. Good leaders act like coaches and good organisations invest in training. Remember, training is not conducted only to improve the skill set of people – it also helps raise their self-esteem.

- *A Sense of Achievement*

Remember the days when you were a kid and were learning to cycle. You fell so many times in the process, sometimes even hurting yourself, but what a thrill it was when you could first learn to balance yourself confidently – just riding away to glory.

A very powerful emotional need in all of us is to achieve. It is a great sense of satisfaction when you say, 'mission accomplished.' For a painter, it is about completing a painting, for a sculptor it is about accomplishing his piece of art and for a mountaineer, it is about reaching the summit. It is, therefore, such a natural desire that everyday at work we set our own targets, achieve them and feel thrilled about it. Those who make it a habit to make steep but achievable targets for themselves, are constantly self-motivated.

Remember, don't set unrealistic or frustrating targets while handling people. This can boomerang and become a very big demotivator. Setting out realistic targets requires experience and knowledge. If you can set workable targets that your teams can achieve, you will be able to keep them motivated. Cakewalks and easy victories are not very satisfying – you also require a challenge, which' you should fight against. Overcoming challenges, gives one tremendous satisfaction. So, setting *realistic* targets – that are neither very difficult to achieve nor a cakewalk, is what is desirable.

- *Recognition and Appreciation*

This is the greatest motivator of all. Each one of us has that inner desire to be appreciated. Public appreciation, loud and clear, is known as recognition. It is a clear booster for one's self-esteem. **We punish very quickly, but don't reward that fast.**

Recognition is the cheapest, best and most lasting incentive. It is '*Sasta, sunder aur tikau*', which means, 'inexpensive, good and lasting.' Everyone wants to be recognised for his work, his contribution and his merits.

Simple things like certificates, medals, prizes, letters of appreciation, a photograph of an achiever on your website make a difference. My son who works for a software company, once organised a ramp show for the employees of his firm. The show went off well and the next day, he called me up, telling me that his CEO had sent him a mail, congratulating him for successfully putting up the show. Since the CEO had taken care to send the mail on the Intranet, all the employees came to know about it. During the lunch break, there were dozens of people who came up to congratulate him. Most of them didn't even know that he had managed the entire show. His day was made. This simple but timely and mature act by the head of the organisation made my son feel so good that he especially gave me a call from Bangalore to inform me about it.

Padma Bhushans, gallantry awards, lifetime achievement awards by organisations and knighthoods are all time-tested morale boosters. These are the objects of desire, that hold great significance for the human ego. A standing ovation at the Oscars is a bigger reward for a person like Steven Spielberg than what money can buy. Take the example of Shammi Kapoor from our own Bollywood or Sidney Poitier from Hollywood. Both of them were almost in tears, thanking God, the audience and the jury, when they were presented with the "Lifetime Achievement Award" – a recognition for dedicated work and contribution to the cinema in their respective countries. What would the cost of fabricating a Grammy, an Oscar or a Filmfare award be? Not more than a few hundred dollars. However, the men and women who have achieved it all – fame, money and material – still vie for a pat on the back.

People are prepared to spend money in order to gain recognition. For example, in the Oscars, one needs to lobby for one's film and reach out to people in the best way possible. This costs money. It was splashed all over the newspapers that *Lagaan* – a film, which was a hit at the Indian box office – was not lobbied properly at the Oscars, not enough money was spent on it!

If Ashutosh Gowarikar, the Director of *Lagaan* was given a hypothetical option of choosing between an Oscar with half the profits sacrificed and keeping all the profits with no Oscar award – I am sure he would have opted for the Oscar. That, is the power of recognition, acknowledgement and appreciation.

Remember, when you handle people, even a pat on the back peps them up. Appreciation at the right place, in front of the right people and at the right time is very effective. As a by-product, you win instant appreciation from the appreciated!

'I can live for two months on a good compliment.'

– Mark Twain

* *Meaning and self-worth*

Each one of us wants to feel that our life matters, we want to live for a reason, a raison d'être – a reason for being, existing. The desire for meaning is a powerful, motivational force. We want to feel significant, contributing to the environment that we live in. That is why most voluntary organisations and Non-Governmental Organisations (NGOs) that work for a cause, often attract people from all stratas of society with a high degree of commitment. Many people who are rich and famous, who have everything that they need, go out and do social work. The human spirit seeks more than a routine, mundane life – it seeks a meaning beyond material and wealth.

If you can get across to people and tell them exactly why they are doing something – you give them a meaning – a reason to work for. People often change a job when they start thinking, 'Why the hell I am doing this job?' When they aren't convinced themselves, they change their job.

> When the Americans were fighting the Germans during the Second World War, they were fighting a war for the British, French and for Europe. They were a third party to the war and were obviously not very convinced what they were fighting for. When General Patton's army defeated the Germans in an offensive and liberated prisoners from concentration camps, the American soldiers saw the pathetic conditions of these ghettos, the torture that the prisoners were undergoing, that had reduced them to skeletons. Patton himself took the soldiers through these camps, showing them the brutality of the Germans and said, 'Boys, this is what we are fighting for.'

If the entire staff in a college is convinced that they are a part of educating the next generation – a noble work – they will feel motivated.

Whatever you do, do your best and strive to boost your self-worth. Let everything that you do, be quality work. **'We as an organisation, believe in quality and customer**

care.' This kind of approach is appealing and lends real meaning to what people do. The movement towards quality consciousness, therefore, acts as a binding force within organisations.

Help people find meaning in what they do. For example, every department within the armed forces is made to feel that they are doing an important job. The logistics guy is as important as a medical man or a sniper sitting in the tree, picking on enemy targets, or a man going in for a bayonet charge. If the pilot who flies an aircraft is important, so is the engineer who maintains it.

- *Stimulation*

Man hates boredom and inactivity. You need to be gainfully employed and duly engaged. That is the reason why many people start a worthwhile activity even after retirement. They may not work for money but they do work for occupation. People are afflicted by 'retirement blues' because of inactivity, rather than a reduced income. Activity motivates us, and that is why outdoor sports are very popular. People often play golf early in the morning because it is an activity, which gives one pleasure and is enjoyable.

In order to avoid boredom, we find innovative ways to keep ourselves engaged. It could be watering the plants or repairing an old gadget at home. Unless an activity is exciting enough, you cannot keep a person riveted to it for long. If the work can be made innovatively stimulating – you can expect people to deliver results from the depths of their hearts.

In fact, people who do not have enough work at the workplace, can become problematic in their behaviour. They can interfere with others' work, making them, in turn, inefficient. **An empty mind is the devil's workshop.**

Adequate load management and keeping everyone happily occupied, can be a good strategy to handle people.

- *Competition*

Having a healthy competition in any environment, can keep people pepped up. Every person sees himself as a winner. If there is no competition, there will be no contest and no winners. This is a losing proposition. In order to handle people you must provide competition. It could be an inter-departmental football match, or the 'most productive' inter-departmental contest. Inter-college water polo matches or a brand equity quiz for the corporates are well fought-out competitions. The capitalistic economy has thrived on healthy competition. The public sector in India, for a long time, had no competition, and hence could not motivate its employees. Today, government banks and Public Sector Undertakings in every field are changing their stance – because they have competition.

- *Faith in Organisations*

When an employee feels that the organisation he works for, will not let him down when he is going through a personal crisis – sure enough, he will be loyal and motivated. Organisations expect employees to work hard and be loyal to them for 365 days of the year. An employee, however, may need organisational support on one odd occasion during his entire tenure. If he is let down at that point, he would definitely feel betrayed. But if the organisation holds his hand when he needs help, – it would have earned his loyalty. Most organisations, unfortunately, do not pay adequate attention to this aspect.

Organisations are built up by people like you and me. Each one of us has to contribute to strengthen this faith amongst the people of the organisation, clearly demonstrating that, 'We all care for each other. We will stand by you when you need us.' **You may not participate in someone's happiness, but you must stand by him during his sorrow.**

The 10 human requirements that we just discussed, that motivate people right from the heart are all interlinked. One often depends on the other. While dealing with people, it is important to keep all of these in mind. Whether you are a supervisor on the shop floor, a marketing manger in a software company, a vice president of a manufacturing company or a CEO of a multinational organisation, these basic requirements apply to all of you and to all those who work for you and work along with you. Each person is an entity and these are the basic human buttons, that when pressed correctly, at the right time, can make a person tick – and that's what you want to accomplish, don't you?

If

'If you can talk with crowds and keep your virtue,
Or walk with Kings – nor lose the common touch,
If neither foes nor loving friends can hurt you,
If all men count with you, but none too much:

If you can fill the unforgiving minute
With sixty seconds' worth of distance run,
Yours is the Earth and everything that's in it,
And – which is more – you'll be a Man, my son!

– Rudyard Kipling

Motivating Your Team

Motivating a group of people can be very interesting and challenging. Although we are talking about group or team motivation, remember that a group consists of people who have individual personalities. In order to keep the entire team together and to take it along, you should keep individual emotional strengths and weaknesses in mind. As a captain of the cricket team, you have to deal with people who are cool, people who are nervous, edgy and short-tempered. You have to deal with players who collapse under pressure and players who perform and shine when the chips are down. For an optimum team performance, you have to get the best out of each team player, putting the right person in the right place at the right time. This is the key to success, as well as keeping everybody motivated. Remember live problems, which a team has to handle, are not as simple as 'tug of war' – just heave together, and you win. Performance has to be delivered over a longer period of time and therefore, the 'sustainability' of motivation becomes a very important parameter – it must last. Lastly, as a team leader, don't only consider the operational or domain strengths of individuals, look at their emotional strengths as well. Therefore, you must be 'emotionally awake' and 'watch and register' the emotional nuances of each of the team members.

'The golden rule is that there is no golden rule.'

– George Bernard Shaw

The basic ground rules for keeping your team motivated are:

- *You yourself, have to be motivated*

To motivate your team, you have to firstly ensure that you are in the right frame of mind, that you are yourself in control and are in an upbeat mood to motivate others. If you can't keep your cool as the captain of the team – don't expect it from others. Remember that each member of the team is looking up to you and observing you more closely than you think they are.

- *Goal-directed motivation*

As the leader of a team, you should be able to clearly identify, define and show a goal – an achievable one – to your team members. Even a mountain goat doesn't climb up without a goal. This is why, in a military operation, defining the 'mission' assumes highest priority and importance.

- *Participation*

You must ensure that each member participates right from the start to finish. Push and prod those who need it, but never shove.

- *Involving and keeping members informed*

The key is to disseminate information. Keep people informed about the progress. Telling them the reason, why you are doing something, is more important than what you are doing.

- *Progress and competence*

Ensure that each member of the team gets an adequate chance to improve his performance. During net practice, look at the bowlers, batsmen and fielders – but don't forget the wicket keeper. Give adequate training to all, pay adequate attention to everyone's need to sharpen his own axe. This is a great motivator.

- *Reward the performer*

We often come across cases of 'blue eyed boys.' You may have your favourites at your workplace, but treat everyone equally as far as possible. No soft corners for anyone please! Soft corners for a few can become rough edges for the rest of the team! Reward people as per their performances. Never reward people just because they are your favourites. This is the first seed sown for sycophancy and the start of organisational politics. Remember, politics starts from the top and is then, often blamed upon the juniors.

- *Treat people appropriately*

Now, this is important. It is not only important to treat people fairly, it is also important to treat people appropriately. Each person must be given his due respect and his due credit. This will generate a lot of respect and regard for the leader.

- *Making a person feel important*

We all have our own egos. We love it if our ego is given a boost. Everyone wants to be an important contributor and make a difference to his organisation. It is related to self-worth on the emotional plane. None of your employees must ever ask himself, 'Am I worthless?' It is important that everyone feels like he is an indispensable part of the entire show. A bowler, a batsman and a wicket keeper – are all important to pick up the World Cup – it is the case of a cricket team playing together and not a shot put competition where individual excellence is on display.

- *Motivational threshhold*

Many people in a team are highly spirited and remain at a high motivational level on their own. Such people rarely require an external 'pep dose.' Then, there are others who require that occasional motivational shot to keep them going. What I am trying to get at, is that each person has a different motivational threshhold or a fuse. As team leader, it is very important for you to identify the personal motivational threshholds of people and handle them accordingly. It acts like a 'key' for that person. Remember, every lock has a key. Find the right one and you can open the lock.

- *A sense of belonging – bond with the best*

To belong to a group gives one a sense of pride and security. Make people proud of being a part of the team, also inculcating the feeling that they belong to an elite group, a team worth bonding with. There are 16 squadrons at the National Defence Academy. The trainee cadets feel proud of belonging to their squadrons and this spirit is retained throughout their service career, during peace as well as war.

- *Strong Organisational Culture*

Organisations, that build strong cultures, motivate people

with a sense of belonging. Good companies like Infosys or IBM, invest time and energy to foster strong cultural bonds amongst their employees.

- *Keep at it*

Motivation is like the air pressure in your car's tyre. You've got to check it out at regular intervals and pump it up every 15 days or so. As group leaders and project heads, don't ever be complacent in the feeling that you have done all that had to be done and that everything is now in place, so the guys are going to be motivated happily ever after. Remember, even inoculations are repeated after certain periods. So, all the methods for motivating people are to be kept in mind and applied in real time, always and all the time.

Keep these 12 principles in mind and use them innovatively. Most of them work on an emotional human plane. If used intelligently and skilfully, they can really change the way organisations work, bringing in harmony, that feel-good factor and high energy levels leading to better productivity.

Till now, I have discussed what influences people, basic needs that motivate them and thumb rules to motivate your team. These are all interlinked and interdependent. All of these put together, give you an understanding of how to handle people on the emotional level and get the best out of them.

> *'Diplomacy is the art of letting someone have your way.'*

> – Daniele Vare

Motivational Criticism

Remember – I had said earlier that dealing with people does not mean being a goody-goody guy all the time. In order to handle people effectively, you've got to sometimes tell them, what they are doing is wrong – a harsh word for this is 'criticism'. There are smart ways of telling a guy that he is wrong, and yet getting the best out of him. This is known as motivational criticism. Here are a few tips to criticise people and yet, motivate them in the bargain.

- *Timing is important*

Don't tell a person that his performance has not been satisfactory when he is going away for the weekend. This can really be demoralising and can spoil his weekend without him achieving anything extra. Let him charge his batteries during the weekend and talk to him on a Monday if you must. Again, someone may come back after a traumatic weekend, say a mishap at home – you must never criticise at this time, it will be inhuman and will have a devastating effect on your relationship with the employee.

- *Criticise privately, not in public*

Never criticise a person in front of others. This is a disaster because you end up humiliating the person.

- *First the positives, later the negatives*

When you have to talk to a person regarding his unsatisfactory performance or anything else that is negative, it is always better to first talk to him about his positives, before telling him about his drawbacks. It is a very commonsensical approach, but most of us hardly ever take it.

- *Be specific*

Don't call a person and say, 'I feel there is a lot of chaos in your department and nothing seems to be moving right!' Now what does that mean? First of all, it is an exaggeration and secondly, it doesn't convey a definite meaning on which someone can take action and make an improvement. Thirdly, it puts a person on the defensive and he tends to defend himself, rather than listen to you. Always be specific and tell a person what exactly is wrong.

- *Never be sarcastic*

Now, this is bad. Never be sarcastic – always approach the problem upfront, in a straight-forward manner. Remember, if someone happens to behave sarcastically with you, it would hurt you the most. It is very bad for interpersonal relations.

- *Criticise, focussing on the mistake, not the person*

Criticising a person may sometimes take a personal hue, which no one would like. Talk only about the problem and not the person.

- *Don't question the intention*

The moment you question a person's intention, it becomes a personal issue. It amounts to questioning a person's integrity – which becomes a very serious matter. It can end up making a mountain out of a molehill, snowballing the situation which is very bad for relationships.

- *Give people the benefit of doubt*

In case a person defends himself and the benefit of doubt in a situation goes to him – let him have it. The point is driven home, but the person leaves with a better taste in his mouth. It amounts to a face-saving measure. Remember that you are conveying a point, but want to keep relations intact – that is the larger interest.

- *Be a coach*

Now, this is seldom done. If you have the right to point out a mistake, you would also have the responsibility of telling the guy how to fix that mistake. Assuming the role of a coach, puts you on a higher pedestal and your team respects you for that.

- *Encouraging a person after the criticism*

Once that shortcomings have been discussed, and the methodology to improve them have been put in place, there is always room to boost the person so that he goes back to work in a better, positive frame of mind. Build his confidence by telling him something pleasant about his personality and other positive achievements. This goes a long, long way in developing his personality.

- *Fix a time for a review*

It is good practice to give a person time to make improvements and get back to you. This in fact, completes the cycle right from the time of criticism, to making an improvement.

- *Praise a person after he has accomplished what you wanted him to*

If someone has made an effort to improve, it is obviously a good idea to say, 'Well done!'

These are practical ways of handling people on a day-to-day basis, getting your point across, yet not hurting anyone.

The do's of social competence

- *Take personal criticism in your stride*

While criticising others is easy, taking personal criticism in your stride requires a brave heart. Personal criticism, I must say, should also be taken in a constructive manner. It can then help make positive changes in your personality. Anupam Kher, a respected Bollywood actor has claimed in many interviews that his wife is his biggest critic. She points out his weaknesses on-screen and he takes it positively, in order to improve his performance. When actors of such high calibre take criticism with a straight face and use it to improve their performance, then why should all of us not try and emulate this behaviour, regardless of the profession that we pursue? In management institutes for instance, an effective method of improving communication skills is by making each student stand in front of the entire batch, make a presentation and take a dispassionate feedback from his peers. This improves performance and also does some good to one's personality – making one ready to take on the world by taking criticism positively.

- *Have the guts to apologise*

You can't be always right – but most of us think otherwise. If you goof up, you know it and others know it too! Most people think that accepting a mistake will make them look small. This is a wrong notion, in fact, accepting your mistake earns you respect from others. If you have been rude to someone, but are prepared to say sorry afterwards, you are showing signs of being magnanimous. **Don't be afraid to say you messed up. People appreciate that in a person.**

Most of us do the wrong thing and on top of it, spend enormous efforts, defending what we did. Saying sorry or being apologetic takes a big heart and lots of guts. But most of us are timid and subsumed by some sort of an inferiority complex which is why, we do not have the guts to say so. You don't have to look apologetic all the time, but there are occasions where you've got to convey it loud and clear that you went wrong. If you do this, you will come out of the situation, a better person who everyone respects.

- *Reading emotional cues and behaving accordingly*

Fancy names for this are 'social analysis', 'adaptability' or 'social intelligence.' It is a great asset to be able to pick up cues from a conversation and find out what the correct response is. Remember, perception is reality – and the way that you conduct yourself or respond to other people's remarks, fixes an impression about you in others' minds. This, in simple terms, is impression management. Is there any point blurting out something stupid that hurts about

10 people around you, just on the pretext of being honest about your feelings? Emotionally intelligent people, in fact, weigh out their words before they speak. They think of the repercussions before they open their mouths. **Diplomacy is thinking twice before saying nothing.**

Those who can master this art of social intelligence are often seen as 'polished' people who are emotionally nourishing and, 'a nice guy to be with.' They leave people in a good mood and make a positive impact on others.

- *Handling the ego in others*

Accept one simple fact – we all have an ego. Hurting somebody on the ego-front can surely get you an enemy for free. This is because the ego is very personal, it is the self-image of a person. There are those who have a big ego (actually a small one) who would make everything a personal issue. Such people are difficult to handle, but they can be easily managed with tact. In fact, if you can handle their ego, the rest, however big will follow. If social analysis tells you that the guy has a big ego, do a bit of 'ego massaging' and everything else will fall in place. These are the 'handle with care' guys who should be handled accordingly. Don't ever feel inferior to them, because remember, bigger the ego, the smaller the man!

- *Trust*

In the context of interpersonal skills, trust is about trusting your team and the team trusting you. Mistrust has its own overheads. You all spend so much time defending, enquiring and reconfirming, that there is little time left for work. In fact, it is very demoralising to work in an environment where there is lack of trust. If you know that your team members will not intentionally let you down – it means you trust them. If you instinctively know that your team members will always act in your best interests – it means you trust them – then you can share your ideas freely with your team. The reverse, therefore, must also be true because trust is not a one-way process. It goes beyond rapport, which is only about getting along and understanding each other's nuances. Trust is at a much deeper level and provides psychological comfort to the entire team. People leave their organisations when they have to always watch their backs as they go about their day's work.

Mistrust in one's organisation leads to the 'you are a thief unless proven otherwise', syndrome. This implies a lack of faith in each other, a lack of belief. Inter-organisational documents, especially the legal ones, can become very lengthy and time-consuming – not serving much purpose. The Japanese make very short documents and use trust instead, to resolve issues if any. In the not-so-distant past, people would make deals and verbal commitments based merely on trust. These were honoured till the very end. People gave their '*zuban*' (their word) and honoured it to the hilt.

We must today, ensure that inter-organisational and intra-organisational trust must be built, as it results in tremendous positive energy in the entire organisation. As the leader of a team or an organisation, you must give the highest priority to 'building bridges of trust.'

- *Involving the people*

There was once a jailer, who had an impeccable track record. He always treated the prison inmates with dignity and was downright honest. One fine day, there was an uprising against him, complaints were made and a petition was sent to the Minister of Jails. The Minister himself was surprised and decided to visit the jail – he went straight to the prisoners to get a first-hand account of things. The prisoners' story went something like this. They told the minister that for the last two weeks, the jailer appeared to have either gone mad or that he had become very sadistic. They said that every morning they were made to stand in a line and dig trenches almost six feet deep. By the time that it was evening, they were asked to fill the trenches again! This was simple punishment and was very frustrating for them.

The Minister was also surprised and annoyed, and he asked the jailer for an explanation. The jailer was not surprised and told him that all he was trying to do, was to locate a faulty water pipeline, which was running in the backyard of the jail. Since the pipeline was 30 years old, they had no blueprint which could pinpoint the alignment of the pipelines – digging and locating the pipeline was, therefore, the only answer!

The jailer did not intend to punish the prisoners. In fact, locating that pipeline would have expedited repairs and improved water supply for the prisoners themselves! This was a case of lack of communication and involving people in the job. The most important aspect of involvement meant telling the team members why they were doing what they were doing.

If as a team leader you have a grand plan – for heaven's sake inform your teammates about the mission.

• *Conflict Resolution*

This is an important skill to develop social competence and leadership. There are many occasions when arguments get out of hand and you need to act as a mediator. It often happens that a very small misunderstanding snowballs into a showdown, which could even result in the breakdown of personal relations. All those who demonstrate maturity in such situations and take the initiative to solve the issue, come out as winners. Resolving conflict is an art, but many of us either don't have the guts to take the bull by its horns, or are indifferent to the situation.

> *'Tact is the ability to tell a man he is open-minded, when he has a hole in his head.'*
>
> – F G Kernan

Bhanu was sitting with his friend who had come in from Nepal when his elder brother entered the house. They did not speak a word to each other and big brother went straight inside, not even wishing his friend. Bhanu's friend asked him who the gentleman was, and was surprised when Bhanu told him that it was his brother. His friend asked him why he was not introduced to his brother. Bhanu told him that they were not on talking terms for the past three years. His friend knew that there was a serious problem between the two, and proceeded to ask Bhanu what exactly the problem was about. Bhanu told him that he maintained a personal diary, which his elder brother had read. This was an unpardonable crime. He had, therefore, stopped speaking to him. Bhanu's friend asked him how was he sure that his brother had read his diary. Bhanu said, 'Because I read it in his diary!' Bhanu's friend was a genuine one. He acted as a mediator, got the two brothers together, and made them patch up and become friends again.

The moral of the story is that we first find faults with others and don't look at our own faults. That is how a conflict starts. Secondly, if there are well-meaning people around, they take the initiative to resolve an issue by acting as mediators.

- *Humour*

Using humour in interpersonal relations is an effective way of getting along with people and generating pep in the air. People who can bring humour into their daily lives by cracking light-hearted jokes at home, at parties or at work, become very popular and are liked by others. This is a natural gift that most of us have but those who don't, can learn to at least laugh at jokes – many don't even do this. You may not always be spontaneous, but you can consciously bring humour into your day-to-day life. So, develop a sense of humour. Bring a little humour into discussions, presentations and gossip. It does help.

The Don'ts of Social Competence

There are many mistakes that we make while handling our relationships with people. But there are a few major ones that can be disastrous, that you must always keep a note of.

- *Right pressure at the right point*

Our late Prime Minister, Mr Rajiv Gandhi, while inaugurating the National Snooker Championship in Delhi, made a very important remark in his speech. He said, 'Politics and snooker are very much similar because in both of them it is important to know how much pressure to apply and at what point.' In fact, the same holds good for interpersonal skills. While handling situations and people, you must know how much pressure to apply to whom and under what circumstances. This is actually the essence of handling people. As a rule of the thumb, never apply more than the required pressure.

- *Hurting others' self-esteem*

If you step on someone's toes accidentally, making him jump with pain – and say sorry, he would most probably forgive you. But if you hurt someone's self-esteem, be rest assured that he would never forgive you, however much you may apologise. No person worth his salt would ever allow you to fool around with his pride and esteem. You must never ever do that.

Public Criticism

'One should keep ones words both soft and tender, because tomorrow you may have to eat them.'

Public criticism sometimes becomes extremely personal. It is insulting and also at times, demeaning. It is always better to call a person in private and talk things over. Public criticism is humiliating and hurts one's self-esteem. There can be exceptions where you need to criticise someone in front of others. This may be the case in a situation where you give more than enough opportunities to someone to improve, but find the same mistakes being repeated time and again. In such a case, the person either does it deliberately, or is just not bothered about what you think or say. You could warn him the last time in privacy, that the next time the firing will be in public – and then you would be well within your rights to thrash it out publicly. This, however, should be used as the last resort, only as an exception, not the rule.

- *Black-and-white mode*

There are people who have strong likes and dislikes for others. They work in the black-and-white mode. It is very difficult to work with people like these. I had a boss who had such strong likes and dislikes. He unfortunately disliked me. My life was miserable, working under him for full three years. Whatever I did, he was sure to criticise. Even when I did something right, he thought I had a 'hidden agenda'. I had no way of proving myself right.

Such bosses or leaders lose out on their teams. They choke half their bandwidth just because of their whims and fancies. Since the boss has declared a chap useless – he becomes just that, useless. This is the worst form of leadership. This leads to the, 'I know that you know that

I know', syndrome, leading the leader and the follower nowhere. So, for heaven's sake, never practise this. If need be, change yourself – upgrade yourself from a black-and-white mode to full colour and see the gradations in people!

Manage Your Mood: It is Contagious

Managing your mood and presenting yourself appropriately in front of others, is very important for interpersonal relations. Remember, no one likes a moron or a foul-mouthed guy. A pleasant personality is what goes in well with people. It is also important to understand that your behaviour has a direct impact on people around you. If you are calm, your team is calm. If you panic or look worried, your team will panic and worry. It is a transmitter-and-receiver mode – you are the transmitter and others are receivers. Moods are very contagious. As a leader, you have to look calm and composed outwardly, even in a crisis.

We are all a part of each other's emotional tool kit. We provide emotional support to each other and are emotional crutches for one another, especially in difficult situations. Lifting your own spirits is an art and lifting the spirits of a group of people around you is a bigger art. If you are conscious about this and manage to influence the mood of your own team, you would be a winner all the way.

Setting the Emotional Tone

There are people who can dominate and set the emotional tone and complexion of an interaction. These are great actors who can influence the emotions of a group and steer conversation the way they want. Whichever side of the argument they are on, they always seem to be right. They can sway and swing the conversation as they like. Remember, it is not only logic that matters, it is also how one puts it across, which is probably more important. When you watch a movie, you know that it is not reality, it is a performance by actors and that you have paid to see it – yet you are so emotionally moved by the film – many times coming close to tears. **Emotions in others can be managed and that is the sign of power and leadership.**

Shaking up People: Shock and Awe

Adolf Hitler didn't rise to power to become the most powerful person of his time by default. He made it happen by design. His political rallies were full of flags and mascots, the buildings had huge flags and Swastikas rolling out of them. He used black, white and red colours to create that awe. His office, where he received visitors was very long, with flags and paintings placed on both sides. A visitor had to walk almost 50 steps in order to reach the Führer's table. Hitler used to sit, looking into the visitor's eyes, watching him walk up nervously towards his table. By the time a person reached the table, he was already under Hitler's authoritarian spell. Half the battle was won before even a word was spoken. He won many political deals and managed his empire with shock and awe. He really shook up people with this style.

This kind of style is never recommended when we deal with people. But when a situation arises where you can't spare the rod – use it. This should, however, never be used in a routine manner.

> *'Friendship is an arrangement by which we undertake to exchange small favours for big ones.'*
>
> – Baron de Montesquieu

Getting Along and Networking

There are many people who label themselves as 'reserved.' They think they mind their own business and are men of few words. This attitude is fine, but minding your own business and staying aloof may not be a great quality. In fact, making friends and getting along with people is a strong trait of successful leadership.

Remember, public relations, networking, getting along with people and making friends, all mean the same thing. Those with a friendly nature, are not only liked by others, they also get more windows of opportunities as they meet new people. This can be seen at the level of international relations, when two nations become friendly with improved trade and business because the heads of state get along well! Somehow, the chemistry between the Indian political leadership and the American powers-that-be didn't work well in the mid-fifties, and India chose to befriend the Russians, who had a totally different ideology! Business between two companies can take an upswing if CEOs hit it off well. I have seen deals come through and government approvals for projects being given a go-ahead on the basis of personal relations, pure and simple.

'To find a friend one must close one eye – to keep him, two.'

– Norman Douglas

Keeping good, friendly relations with your peers is always helpful. A marketing head may think, 'I am doing a good job and meeting my targets, why should I keep good relations with the finance head?' Logical as it may sound, it is actually wrong thinking. If he puts up a proposal in a board meeting, chances are that his idea would be shot down by the finance head if he is totally disconnected to the finance department. Whether it is a small project leader and his team, or CEOs dealing with large multinational corporations or the heads of states – getting along with one another, hitting the right chord and reaching workable comfort levels, is a very important requirement for progress and success.

Leaders and Social Art

In order to be a good leader, you should be good at the art of handling people because leaders lead people and that is their bread-and-butter. The best of engineers, finance wizards and management graduates fail as leaders, because they can't handle people. All these fellows crack thousands of logic-seeking problems, crunch millions of numbers and solve hundreds of case studies related to the business environment, but they unfortunately have no formal training in handling people or in creating good human relations. **Without emotions you can manage, but cannot lead.**

The duties that a leader must assume and the qualities he must demonstrate.

Leading people is an art, leading people is a responsibility and leading people is not easy. A leader must earn and command respect, and in order to be able to do that, a lot is expected of him.

An important trait of a good leader is, that people should be able to confide in you and should therefore, trust you. They should have faith in you, in your capabilities and should look up to you. You should in a crisis, be able to hold their hand and if required, even provide a shoulder for them to cry on.

These capabilities must be demonstrated and are applicable at all levels of leadership across the board, whether one is a project team leader, the captain of a cricket team, the CEO of a large firm, or the leader of a nation.

In order to be able to develop leadership into a manageable art, I would like to explain what is expected of you. Read on.

- *Group Harmony*

Keeping the team together, is the foremost job of a leader. Taking the maximum out of each member individually and collectively as a team, is in essence, the job of a leader. People have a varied range of talents and taking advantage of all the talents of all the members, can make the teamwork wonders. Putting the right man on right job at the right time, is the name of the game. Let everyone contribute to the effort. Whether it is cricket or a marketing campaign, it works the same way.

As a leader, you should be able to persuade people, yet avoid conflicts from taking place. You also have to become a mediator during interpersonal conflicts amongst members of your team. **Remember, your team's performance is not calculated by the average IQ of the group, which is the sum total of the talent and skill that the group possesses.** Performance is a direct function of group harmony. Social harmony and getting along with one another, make a group more productive than others.

Excitement levels of members differ. If you have an extremely smart guy who dominates the group, the rest of the group will then, not be able to contribute their bit. The energies of such dominating and over-zealous members must be rightly channelised. Then, there are the 'deadweights', who don't participate at all. They need to be pushed. Get them moving. Then, there are the fence-sitters who need to be prodded to get optimum performance out of them. Leaders must build consensus over tricky issues and get the team to agree to a common thought process, wherever required. If you can carry your team along, half the battle is won and the other half becomes easy.

- *The leader as a group's emotional guide*

When everything is fine, the team performs well on its own. It is only when the chips are down, that the leader has to play a critical role. A leader has to be his group's emotional guide. Remember that the team is looking up to you. Your behaviour has a direct impact on the performance of the team. If you remain hopeful, the team is hopeful, if you look positive, the team becomes positively-inclined. The leader drives the collective emotions of the team.

- *Where must you use the rod?*

An automobile engineer's car once broke down on the highway. Though he tried his best, he couldn't manage to fix it. A roadside mechanic came up to him, ready to help. He asked the automobile engineer to sit in the car while he did something to get the car going. The mechanic took a rod and banged the car on its rear – it started moving! The car owner asked him how much he should pay him for his service and the mechanic said, Rs 500. 'What?' exclaimed the automobile engineer, 'Rs 500 for just using the rod?' 'No, not for just using the rod, but for using it at the right place.' The moral of the story is, while using a rod is a technique, you must also know when, where and how hard to use it – if you must.

- *Providing a conducive work atmosphere*

The leader's job is to extract the maximum out of his team. The right atmosphere, where people find encouragement, satisfaction and happiness can go a long way in helping you get the best out of your boys. Remember, it is not always possible to have your entire team excited about the work. There are many who work simply because they have to earn a living – which is no crime. But, you must provide an environment where people can contribute as much as they can. This approach to a large extent, compensates for any employees' lack of passion towards his work. **Never try to change a person, rather, create an environment where a person wants to change for you.**

- *Building relationships beyond the organisation*

Teams never work in isolation, even large organisations have to interact with the rest of the business environment. There is, therefore, a need for leaders to have a good working relationship with their peers at the same level and also with people who matter at the top. This is what I call horizontal and vertical relationship management. If you get along well with your peers on the horizontal level, inter-departmental issues between your department and others will be easily sorted out. If you get along with your top management, approvals, sanctions and projects will be smoother to be pushed through. Remember, it is in the larger interest of the team that a leader should get along with the bosses on top, because the department benefits from this.

- *I want to hold your hand*

The President of India, His Excellency, Dr APJ Abdul Kalam, while addressing students of management institutes at Symbiosis, narrated a very interesting incident that explains an important trait of a leader.

> Dr APJ Abdul Kalam, a veteran scientist of international repute was the Project Director for the prestigious SLV Project at the Indian Space Research Organisation (ISRO). The satellite launch was to be conducted on 19 August 1979 and as per norms, the countdown began 24 hours in advance. All systems were checked and found functional, therefore, the final countdown began on the evening of the D-day, 19 August 1979.

Just eight seconds before take off, the computer displayed a fault and a signal for 'mission to be aborted.' As Project Director, he consulted his team of six scientists and tried to analyse the fault. After the analysis, the team came to the conclusion that it was a minor fault, which the systems would be able to take care of during the flight. Dr Kalam gave the 'go ahead' signal and the SLV rocket took off, only to land in the sea within a short while! Mission failed! The whole world watched this happen and the responsibility for the entire mission lay squarely on Dr Kalam's shoulders.

Prof. Satish Dhawan was the Chairman, ISRO, at that time and was Dr Kalam's immediate boss. After this fiasco, Prof. Satish Dhawan came to Dr Kalam's cabin and told him, 'Let us go, there is a Press conference.' During the conference, there was a barrage of questions from the domestic as well as the international Press and they were concerned about the wastage of so much public money. Professor Dhawan answered each of those awkward and embarrassing questions in the best possible manner – taking the full brunt of the firing from the Press.

Eight months later or so, Dr Abdul Kalam was once again Project Director for the same project and this time, the rocket did take off! It was 'mission accomplished.' Prof. Satish Dhawan, once again, came to fetch Dr Abdul Kalam for the Press conference but he said, 'This is your victory – now you address the Press conference.' What a leader Prof. Dhawan must have been! It was a victory for the nation and the whole world was watching. India was watching. Prof. Dhawan gave Dr Abdul Kalam his due at the time of victory! When the chips were down, he took the brunt of the blame and held the hand of the Project Director.

This is what is expected of a leader – can you rise to this level? If you can, you are the ultimate leader.

Leadership Styles

Very often, I have heard people referring to their particular style of leadership, which implies that most people develop and use only one style of leadership during the course of their careers. Whatever the situation, whatever the person, whatever the time, they have an unflinching style – a style that they are proud of and a style, that they are comfortable with. There are people who have a dominating style – they set steep targets and make people chase those. Then there are leaders, who act like guides and teachers. How can a uniform style fit all situations – and on top of it, be successful? **A good leader must use leadership styles, as an efficient mechanic uses tools from his toolbox.**

'If the hammer is the only tool that you have, you will treat everything like a nail!'

Can you use a wrench to hammer a nail or a screwdriver to tighten a nut? You must be nuts, if you do.

In the same manner, different styles can be used in different situations. I will now, briefly cover eight styles of leadership, that can be used, as and when required.

- *A visionary's style*

This kind of a leader would have the approach of shared goals. He would make a good vision and a mission for the organisation and clearly show it to his team. He would make people see it as a collective goal – which becomes the driving force. This is a good style when a project is initiated or a new organisation is born and has to take off.

- *The style of a coach*

Here, the leader acts as a coach, telling people how to do things. He demonstrates how things are done and corrects you when things go wrong. It is a teacher-pupil leadership style. This generates a lot of respect for the leader, but needs the leader to be in the know of things – many times, he should know the details in order to be a coach and a teacher.

- *A pace-setter's style*

Such a leadership style sets high-end targets and chases people so that they chase targets. This style is not sustainable over a long period of time. If done for too long, without a break, it could lead to individual as well as organisational burnout.

- *The style of team builders*

This style builds on making the organisation strong and requires organisational acumen on the part of the leader to be successful. Such a style can be applied in tandem with any other style. Such people groom individuals as well as the teams, eventually making task force-oriented organisations.

- *Democratic leadership*

Whatever we may say, democracy has been the most successful methods of governance across the world. Military rule, communism, et al. have never been able to match up to democracy, that takes everyone along. Similarly, when it comes to individual leadership, taking people along in a democratic way is a good style of handling a team. It is in this way, that a leader listens to the views of all team members, before taking a decision. The decisions are more or less, made by consensus. This should not be misconstrued as a weakness of the leader. It is in fact, a strength of sorts, when you listen to people and take their views seriously before arriving at any major decisions.

- *The autocratic style*

Then, there are people who want to bulldoze every project. They use the rod and use it hard. This is a style, which should be used sparingly – in fact, only when there is no other choice. Such a style could usually be used when the company is doing very badly, when the situation is chaotic and things need to be straightened out – at whatever cost. This is best used in company turnarounds. It could also be used when you inherit a bad legacy, handed over to you by someone who has messed up an organisation, including its culture. But use it as a last resort!

- *Charismatic leadership*

Charisma is God's gift. It is highly personality-oriented, where a person is able to cast a spell on the people by his sheer presence. People are awe-struck by such personalities. It is difficult to develop this style, because this is a gift-related style. But with a large span of experience, a few of us may be able to rise up to this level of influencing people with our presence. People like Winston Churchill, Indira Gandhi, and John F. Kennedy successfully carried the masses along with them.

- *Leading from the front*

Leading from the front not only requires guts, it also requires a good grip of the job and most of all – the will to push yourself into the middle of every situation. Such leaders are omnipresent and omnipotent. This style is highly demonstrative. It's like a skipper leading his men into battle – going through the minefield first. This style of leadership is also instinctive and very rewarding because it has a positive effect on the people whom you lead.

Situational Leadership

The eight styles of leadership given above are distinct and can be very effective methods of leading organisations, teams and people. A leader should never use one style – which he says is his own – throughout his career or his tenure in an assignment. **Use these styles as tools to fix specific problems. Change your style as per the situation.** Style could change four times in a month, or even three times during the course of a day. For example, in case you are discussing a matter, which you feel requires consensus, then use a democratic method in a meeting in the morning. Be a coach in the afternoon to the marketing team which needs to learn the ropes before launching a new product and be a visionary when you address a meeting of all the employees in the evening, telling them about a new department which is being constituted for Business Process Outsourcing, as that is where everybody's future lies! You must change your style as per the situation, wear a different hat for a different job – and it will do wonders. But with any of these styles, you must remember to apply all the basics of social competence that we discussed in this chapter and then see, how effectively you can handle people and situations.

IN A NUTSHELL

Handling people is a complex, yet an interesting job. It is also essential for all of us – regardless of the profession that we pursue – to deal with people effectively. In order to do this, you must keep in mind the factors that influence people at a macro level, be it faith, philosophy or oratory skills. To know the pulse of the people, you must remember the ten desires of humans, that are great motivators and use them intelligently while motivating your team. There are occasions when you need to tell someone that he has gone wrong. We have discussed a simple, yet workable method to criticise and yet motivate a person. Use it – it is very effective. Follow the simple do's and don'ts of social competence that have been described and you will win people's respect, feel more comfortable handling them, and above all, find yourself confident in every situation. Keep your own mood in check and always remind yourself that it is important to dominate the emotional tone of an argument, if you want people to listen to you.

Making friends is an extremely important part of our lives and those who are poor at it, must make a genuine effort to reach out and make friends. Begin at the work place. You have a large number of people around you, while you work. Then you can work your way up in the neighbourhood at home. Don't be a social recluse – it helps no one.

Leadership is nothing, but about handling people appropriately. The first job of a leader is to provide a conducive atmosphere, so that everybody can contribute to it. The second important one is to ensure emotional harmony, invoking a sense of belonging in the team. Build trust and always hold the hand of a team member, whenever he needs it. People must trust you and you must trust your team. Don't get stuck with one style of leadership. This would curtail your overall potential to get things done. Become a situational leader by bringing in the style that best suits the situation.

'It is the mark of an educated mind to be able to entertain a thought without accepting it.'

Your Personal Road Map

1. Promise yourself, that you will make genuine efforts to make more personal contacts within the organisation that you work for.

2. What confidence building measures will you take and demonstrate, so that the people around you have faith in you? Write down at least three of them.

3. Write down five concrete steps that you would take to motivate people around you at home or at the workplace.

4. Make a conscious effort to bring humour into your day-to-day life.

5. Promise yourself that you will make a conscious effort to appreciate people at home and at the workplace.

6. Promise yourself that you will treat people appropriately.

7. If you make a mistake, have the courage to apologise and say that you are sorry.

8. Try and develop the habit of reading emotional cues that you get from people around you.

9. Promise yourself that you will always keep communication channels open and involve people around you in any task that you plan.

10. Promise yourself that you will take the initiative to clear any misunderstanding that takes place between you and your colleagues, family members or friends.

8

Let the Heart Rule the Head

The 'Catch 22' of Emotional Intelligence

'It is with the heart that one sees rightly, what is essential is invisible to the eye.'

THE CHANGING ENVIRONMENT

In the last 30 years or so, there has been a tremendous change in how business is done. From typically large, monolithic hierarchical manufacturing units, businesses have shifted to service-oriented, flat organisations.

Privatisation and liberalisation in the developing countries, coupled with globalisation, has on the one hand, given more opportunities to a local worker, but has, on the other hand, brought in fierce competition for local business. Whether it is about fast food chains or higher education, no business has any boundaries today. Information Technology and high-end telecom infrastructure have also impacted our lives and literally shrunk the world. Cheaper labour in the third world along with communications, has given a boost to call centers and Business Process Outsourcing (BPO) boom. The customer is the king and consumer expectations are at their peak today.

All this means opportunities, glitter and gold. All this also means pressure, ambition and stress.

Teamwork today, has become very important for 'deliverables.' Handling a software project, running a profitable fast food chain or producing a soap for a TV Channel, all require good, dedicated workers who can perform as a team. In order to be ahead of the competition, it is important that your team should be able to perform better than that of your competitor's. All this has brought human performance to the forefront and the old adage, 'man behind the gun', is more relevant today than it was ever before.

Looking at the world scenario, boundaries are now being redefined. Religions and cultures are instrumental in realigning loyalties amongst nations. Caste, colour and creed are still as important as they were a century ago, if not more. People still hate each other on these parameters.

The Stress Mess

With so much happening around us and so much to be achieved in terms of materialistic gain, stress levels at work, home and schools are bound to increase. People are becoming ruthless at work. They are pushing and prodding the workforce, even beyond tolerance levels. Higher the stakes, higher the stress. These are the circumstances, under which we all work today.

Working with Your Heart

Many of us feel that bringing emotions into our work or treating people with a smile will make us look soft in front of our subordinates. Some people argue that if you are nice to your employees, it will be difficult to take hard decisions when required. Managers feel that their work demands that they work with their heads and not their hearts. Keeping a stiff upper lip and always keeping people on their toes while they work, doesn't improve productivity. On the contrary, not only does it put an upper limit on how much an organisation can achieve, it also kills creativity, initiative and that extra 'zing' that is expected from an employee. The role of a manager has changed today. You can no longer afford to have nasty bosses, foul-mouthed supervisors or insensitive employers. People will not only under-perform – they would leave you and go elsewhere.

In the words of His Excellency, the President of India, Dr APJ Abdul Kalam, the scene has changed today and a leader is not a commander but a coach, not a director but a delegator, not a manager but a mentor.

Remember, all these are transitions on the emotional plane.

All of these are equally important while dealing with one another at home too. Understanding each other's feelings, a little give-and-take and being considerate to others, goes a long way in keeping marriages going. In fact, basic emotional deficiencies like being rigid, rude and over-demanding are some very common, rudimentary but very important reasons for discord and divorces. Of late, it has become a phenomenon in Asean countries and also in India, that young couples, after a year's marriage, file for divorce because they say, 'We are not compatible.' This is a new addition in vocabulary. A good word to learn, but a bad one to practice. When husbands and wives both work, they bring home their 'files', if not physically, at least mentally: and that adds fuel to the fire. We must learn to leave our offices behind whenever we come back home and vice versa. It is difficult, but it is possible.

Let us understand that there is a difference between being emotionally understanding and being 'emotionally timid' while getting work done from people. You can be polite, yet firm. You don't have to be sarcastic to get your point across. You can be considerate and yet not get taken for a ride. You can show compassion, but it shouldn't mean that you are timid. Decency should not reflect weakness. Emotions must, therefore, be intelligently applied.

- Be angry, but never insulting – be in control of yourself.
- Be considerate – but don't get taken for a ride.

- Show compassion – but not beyond a point so as to compromise efficiency.
- Be polite – yet be firm.

Leadership is not domination, but the art of persuading people to achieve. If you are attuned to those whom you deal with, are able to handle disagreements without letting them escalate, achieve flow states for yourself and your team, you are sure to be a winner.

Most importantly, if you put your heart into the job, people notice and people follow your example.

Emotions, Feelings and Decisions

If five people are standing on a railway track and a train approaches, is it right to divert it onto a track where there is only one person? Most of us would say yes – do it. But what if we ask, would it be a good idea to push a person onto the track to prevent the train from killing five people? The answer in this case would be 'no'. Different responses for the same principle – 'sacrifice one life to save five.' Our brain handles information differently than how a computer does. If a computer was presented with these two situations, the answer could have been 'yes' in both the cases, because it sees the numbers and not the situation in the real sense – it arrives at decisions without emotions.

Heartless Decisions

Many of us feel that emotions have no role to play in decision-making and more so, they have no role at all when business-related decisions are made. They often feel that the fictitious character, Mr Spock, in the famous TV serial *Star Trek* who has no emotions, is able to take the right decisions because he is cold, calculating and 'hyper-rational.' This means that people who are devoid of emotions and are heartless, can take hard-nosed, decisions. This also implies that feelings and emotions have no place in intelligence and muddle up our picture of a situation.

This approach compares the human mind to a computer, that can churn and handle data very efficiently. This 'synthetic and surgical' approach doesn't work when we deal with live situations, involving people – situations that are much more complex than what a computer can handle. Since our decisions are not only based on number-crunching, feelings have a major role in thinking and decision-making. The above example of 'sacrifice one life to save five', shows that emotions do play an important role in taking decisions. Emotions, in fact, support the decision-making process.

Every decision that we take, somehow affects someone directly or indirectly. If you expand your business, it affects some people, if you shut down a branch, it affects others. If you buy new machinery, it affects still other people.

Remember, we are looking for 'human' solutions. In war games – which are computer-simulated situations on the battlefield – if you don't take the morale of the forces into account, the entire model will give you a distorted picture. The capability to fight, is measured with numbers like How many tanks? How many guns? Or how many aircraft? It may not give one an idea of the actual capacity to fight, if the men in uniform do not want to fight! And it happens that way in live situations as well.

The Indian Army could take 93,000 soldiers of the Pakistani Army as Prisoners of War (PoW) in 1971, with their complete war machinery intact, not because the Pakistani ground forces did not have the military capability to fight. They didn't put up a fight because they simply didn't want to fight. There was no will to fight. If Mr Spock is given the same data and asked to analyse it – he would never be able to understand – why the Pakistanis surrendered, as Spock has no feelings to help him understand others' feelings. He would, therefore, be dumbstruck!

Battles of the Heart

Spock-like thinking will never be able to analyse how a person like Mahatma Gandhi could bring the British Empire onto its knees without physical fight. Ask Mr Spock how Adolf Hitler could raise Germany from nothing to becoming the mightiest nation in the 1930s and he would not be able to provide a viable answer. The Americans lost to Vietnam despite their military superiority, because they were fighting a third party war. There were no feelings, as it was somebody else's war. The LTTE fought and is still fighting the Sri Lankan forces because they 'feel' that they are fighting for a cause which is theirs. Whichever way you look it, the heart is at the heart of the matter.

Bad Bosses-A Pain in the ...

To quantify the ramifications of emotional deficiencies like a foul mouth, over-criticism or sarcasm may be difficult, but one can say with certainty that these lead to low productivity, bitterness, lack of respect and trust amongst the people in any organisation.

As if life is not difficult enough, we add to other people's pain, sometimes deliberately, most of the times, inadvertently. People with a span of control, whom one calls bosses, can create havoc in organisations by just being bad to their subordinates or being uncaring towards their needs. Now listen to this example:

My mother was sick and hospitalised in Delhi and I was stationed near Chandigarh. I required leave to visit her and promptly requested leave. My boss, who wanted to deny me leave, called me and showing great sympathy, gave me a practical piece of advice. He said that my mother was in the hospital and that it was now the doctors and nurses who were to do the job. What would I achieve by going to Delhi? He was trying to reason out something with me, that was so unreasonable. I did go on leave, but thereafter, lost all respect for him.

Such bosses and even peers are known as a pain in the neck. Let us understand that a pain anywhere, is a pain. Such people are never liked, never respected and are unacceptable as leaders by the rank-and-file.

If you are somewhere close to this, let me ring the warning bell for you – better change now than never. You will not let your team reach its ultimate potential and that will ensure that you never reach the heights, which you can. **Remember; people don't quit jobs, they quit bosses!**

There was a bad boss and nobody liked him in the organisation. People were, in fact, fed up of him.

One day, one of his subordinates was teaching his son at home and during the English lesson, the boy asked him the difference between a disaster and a catastrophy. His father answered 'One day, my boss went fishing in a boat and we learnt that the boat had capsised and that the boss got drowned. This was a disaster, The next day, we came to know that he had come out alive. Now this was a catastrophe.'

There are bosses who are over-critical, they can't get their point across in a manner, which is palatable. Such bosses create an atmosphere full of tension, putting people on the defensive, making them uncooperative, workers who refuse to learn and most of all, evade responsibility. Criticism more than what is desired, is far ahead of personality struggles, lack of appreciation and even pay-scales, as a factor for dissatisfaction and employees quitting a job.

'Good breeding consists in concealing how much we think of ourselves and how little we think of the other person.'

– Mark Twain

How to Handle a 'Pain in the Neck'

There are, unfortunately people, who refuse to change and many times don't realise that they need to change their attitude and become more considerate towards their subordinates. We sometimes have to put up with such people. In order to handle situations and people who are over-critical, one has to change the way one looks at things. Many times, it could be a case of bad subordinates also. The following points could be handy:

- *Keep your cool*

Retaliation is not always the best policy. Once in a while, the boss can lose his cool. It is better to keep your own reactions in check. It pays in the long run.

- *Evaluate his mental state*

He also may have his pressures and compulsions. After all, he is human. He also reports to someone. These soothing thoughts can help and many times, you will see that such thoughts are true.

- *See his point of view*

You can't always be right. Listen carefully and see the other man's point of view. He may be right in a way.

- *Don't defend yourself if you are wrong*

Our defence mechanism gets over-energised when someone points a finger at us. 'How can I be wrong?' we think. Many times, we unnecessarily put up a false defence because we do not want to admit that we are wrong. This is one thing which can stonewall you from the other person and the situation simply snowballs, and gets out of hand.

- *Accepting your mistake and saying sorry*

If you are wrong, the best thing is to admit your mistake and apologise. This defuses anger in the other person straight away.

- *The opportunity to improve*

Take it as a constructive feedback and make it a point to improve upon your performance.

- *Take it positively*

You can always take criticism positively. This saves the day and a lot of heartburn.

Handling People with Care

If you make it a point to look at people as 'fragile' commodities with a visible placard around their neck 'handle with care', you would never go wrong in maintaining relations. Showing compassion, treating everyone with dignity and providing support whenever someone needs it, go a long way in earning respect and building relations that last.

Let me tell you that caring genuinely for your team earns you unparalleled loyalty.

> *'I believe every person has a heart and if you can reach it, you can make a difference.'*
>
> – Uli Derickson

I was once preparing a very important presentation for my organisation, which had to be given in front of a large audience. Our survival depended on this critical presentation. I was to make the entire presentation on my own, but seeing its importance, my boss had gone through it a couple of times while we were on our mock runs.

A night before the final day of presentation, I got terrible news of a mishap at home. A very close relative of mine had died.

I was perplexed and shaken by this news, but at the same time, understood the gravity of the situation for my organisation, if the presentation didn't go well. I had to leave by the next flight, if I was to make it on time. I gave a call to my boss late at night and explained to him the situation. His reply was immediate, 'Virender, I am very sorry to hear this news. Just hand over the presentation to me and push off on leave – I will take care and should be able to handle the presentation myself.' I felt very bad about putting my boss in a tight spot. I went to his place on the way to the airport, handed him the entire stuff and left.

In such a situation, no boss would have allowed his employee to go on leave. But in this case, my boss handled me with care, taking the entire responsibility upon himself, not showing the slightest hesitation while doing so. When I returned from leave, I learnt that he had sat through the night single-handedly and had gone over the complex presentation himself. It of course, went off well. He earned my respect, as well as gratitude – which I can't forget till date – a perfect leader and a gentleman.

Prejudice, Partiality and Hatred

> *'Evil draws men together.'*
>
> – Aristotle

One thing that is evenly distributed over all of mankind is 'discrimination.' Call it prejudice, partiality, bias or even hatred, it unfortunately exists in some form or the other, between one section of society and the other. Go back into history and you will be able to pick up umpteen number of examples to prove how man has treated man in the most beastly of ways possible.

The Dividing Factors

There are some well-defined parameters along which prejudice, partiality and hatred play their part.

• *The religious divide*

Religion has, in fact, divided the world into various pockets today. Religion, which is supposed to unite people, has become the greatest dividing factor. It has become the biggest motivator for terrorism, killing, bias and discrimination amongst people. So strong is the communal feeling, that blind faith has made people blind. Countries are today aligned and support each other on policies, that have their roots deeply in religion, and not ideologies. Democracies support dictators and communists support the non-aligned on the basis of religion.

• *The colour divide*

We humans exist in all races and colours – white, yellow, brown and black. We discriminate against each other on the lines of the colour of our skin. Racial discrimination between whites and blacks (browns included) has been the most predominant and prominent issue, the world over. Mahatma Gandhi felt so strongly about this in South Africa, that he left his practice and his job to come back to India to fight for his rights, and in the bargain won freedom for the country.

• *The caste divide*

This has been the biggest divide of our society in Asia in general, and India in particular. Whether they are Brahmins and Sudras or Rajputs and Bishnois, there have been constant feuds and fights amongst the castes. Gautam Buddha fought against this system of discrimination and the 'untouchables.' He accepted one and all into the fold of Buddhism.

Prejudice is not an opinion, it is an attitude, which encompasses contempt, dislike and loathing.

In the 1960s, the *Encyclopaedia Britannica* described Black people as, 'Woolly haired people having dark skin, sometimes almost black, broad noses and a rather small brain in relation to their size'! Today, 40 years later, such a definition would be shocking and unacceptable.

Prejudice can vary from the 'garden variety' where people just dislike a community to a very high degree of hatred. The level of hatred demonstrated towards Americans by some Muslims can be analysed from the following statement:

'The killing of Americans and their civilian and military allies is the religious duty of each and every Muslim . . . We with God's help call on every Muslim who believes in God's, to kill Americans and plunder their money whenever and wherever they find it.

The 11 September attack gave a harsh lesson to these arrogant people for whom freedom is but for the white race . . . God willing, America's end is near.

– Osama Bin Laden

These are the pent-up feelings of peoples against peoples which show that prejudice varies from the subtle to an extreme form in society.

Germans hated Jews through the 1930s and the1940s. Six million Jews were systematically killed on the basis of prejudice and hatred. That was the time when anti-Semitism was at its peak. The irony of it is that Adolf Hitler, who started this hate campaign and masterminded the killings, was himself not a pure German. According to his family tree, he was one-fourth German, one-fourth Pole, one-fourth Austrian and one-fourth Jew!

Why this Prejudice?

We learn to dislike people early in life. That is why, these feelings get so strongly embedded in us and we cannot get rid of these easily. It almost becomes a reflex action. It is difficult to eradicate these feelings even in adults, who know it is wrong to harbour them. Whites hating blacks, Indians hating Pakistanis, Germans hating Jews – these emotions are formed in childhood, while the reasons that are used to justify them, come later. If Indians and Pakistanis sit down and think, they will realise that they are the same flesh and blood, but on two different sides of two political systems. Indians and Pakistanis eat the same type of food, wear similar clothes and speak almost similar languages. They belonged to the same nation 50 years ago – and yet, this hatred. **We have forgotten the 5,000 years of togetherness and are thriving on the last 50 years of separation and hatred for each other!**

A recent study involving students from a large number of universities revealed how distorted perceptions – which could be preconceived notions – can be. When asked about Negroes, 84 per cent students described them as superstitious and 75 per cent labelled them as lazy! seventy-nine per cent of the same group opined that Jews are shrewd. The human mind treats humans like apples and oranges, thinking with the aid of categories. These categories once formed, are the basis of normal pre-judgement.

How many of us knew that Jews when forced to flee their land 2,500 years ago were not allowed to work as artisans or farmers in the new regions where they fled to? They were only allowed money-lending. So, people hated them because they thought that Jews were lazy and shrewd and didn't want to work hard like farmers. And then came the perception of Jews fleecing people through money-lending. This was not by choice, but was a by-product of restrictive laws! In the 1930s and 1940s, so much hatred was generated against them, that 6 million Jews were killed. **A lie spoken a hundred times, becomes the truth.**

At a personal level, low self-esteem leads to discrimination. People who have low self-esteem, or a complex, try and show others down on the basis of group belonging. A person may not be good at all, but just because he belongs to a group, which he feels is superior than other groups, he shows his superiority, showing down people from other groups.

People also feel very 'clannish.' Old boys' associations in schools and colleges try to help out one another, guys from the same region, speaking same language, do favours to each other. Team spirit and camaraderie does not mean outright favouritism!

The Role of Organisations Against Prejudice

Discrimination and prejudice is done at a personal level or at the organisational level. At a personal level, it could mean that a manager while recruiting, rejects people from a particular community outrightly because he dislikes them. It becomes very organised in case it has the patronage of the whole organisation. Such an organisation can never survive in today's competitive world.

Politics starts from the top. This must, therefore, be stopped at the highest level in organisations.

Making people aware about the negative fallouts of such behaviour is a good starting point against discrimination. Empathy is also an answer to, 'How do they feel about it?' or 'How will you feel if you were in their place?' This kind of approach also does one a lot of good. It generates a positive feeling towards the particular person or community, which is being discriminated.

Such cases should anyway, not be tolerated and should be dealt with a heavy hand.

Remember, if we can fight against prejudice, discrimination and hatred, we would be living in a better and safer world, and a more conducive environment. Don't forget that you may be in a good position today, but this doesn't mean that you will not be at the receiving end of prejudice tomorrow.

Intuition and the Gut Feeling

Call it the sixth sense, the gut feeling, or beyond the rational; there are occasions when we get a strong inner feeling about a project's success, about a business deal going the right way, or a hunch about something that is going to happen – good, bad or ugly. A large number – close to 90 per cent – of Nobel Prize winners, have attributed their success to intuition.

When you go to buy a house, you look at a number of them and reject, them, but suddenly when you enter a house on sale and get that feeling which says – yes this is it – you go for it. It is a feeling, which comes, maybe, from all the accumulated experiences that we have, and when all the data put up in front of us, cannot help us make a decision. This inner feeling helps us do it.

Management tools and methods can analyse data, provide solutions and help in decision-making where things are pretty much simple. 'If this, then that', kind of situations are limited to simple situations. But today, things are very complex and situations are very dynamic. The exact modelling of a problem is not possible. In such circumstances, managers, especially at higher levels, call upon their intuitive responses to take a decision. They also, I assume, pick up the 'tell-tale' marks, that are mostly invisible, but can be seen or heard somewhere deep down.

This boils down to listening to your heart. When something is not OK, your heart tells you so by activating 'that funny feeling' in your stomach. That is why it is called the GUT feeling.

Intuition is now regarded as a natural ability of the creative process, decision-making and problem-solving. There are CEOs from multinationals who can walk around a manufacturing plant and by just talking to people and noticing their body language, can come to the conclusion whether the plant is doing a good job or not. All these feelings of judging situations and people are backed up by experience and knowledge.

Holistic thinkers mix rational analysis and intuition to come to their conclusions.

The Ace of Hearts

When we are in authority, we all try to be over-bearing and think that we can get the people moving. We also feel that we have a right to motivate people. Have we thought of influencing people who are outside the radius of our influence? These are the people who we have no authority over. Motivating people who are not under our authoritative spell in essence, is the test of our motivational skills.

If you can create an atmosphere of awe around you, such that people from other departments come and discuss their problems with you, seek your advice and guidance – then you have arrived. When I use the word 'awe', I mean genuine respect for yourself, where people look up to you for your values and admire you as a person.

When you are genuine in all this and sincerely mean to do good to all those who come in contact with you, you become the ace of hearts.

Gandhi could motivate millions to move against the British, when he had no authority. He was neither the President, nor the Prime Minister.

Try and develop this habit of influencing people who are not under your authority. It is a great learning experience. If there is a group of 10 agitated people who are not prepared to listen or to let go, and you can put some sense into them as a third party – it is a great victory. All of this can be done only at an emotional plane – authority has no role to play in such situations. Try to use your emotional skills to connect with and correct people, and communicate with them at every opportunity that you get. Do it in the society that you live in, in your neighbourhood, the different departments of your company and even in public places.

If two volunteers come to your house to collect donation for a concert being held to help AIDS patients, try and connect with them on an emotional level, give them not only some money, but also advice which will help their efforts.

Many of us don't, most of us won't, some can't but let me tell you that all of us can. If you make these small efforts to touch people's hearts, you will succeed like you never did.

Also remember that whenever you take a decision, there should always be a balanced approach – a balance between the heart and the head, kind of 50–50. In most situations, we need to take a decision, which takes care of the rational and emotional aspects. There are, however, situations where you need to be compassionate. Then, you've got to listen to your heart more than the head. And then there are instances where you must use the rod – here you need to listen to the head more than your heart – swing towards the head. Remember to use a good mix as the situation demands. Take care that you don't go to the extremities of the spectrum – only the heart or only the head, this can be dangerous and harmful for you, the other party and the situation itself.

IN A NUTSHELL

The business environment today, has changed. Technology and competition have opened up new avenues. Teamwork and human resources are at a premium in today's turbulent times. Religions and cultures have great importance in binding people and nations. There is stress at home as well as the work place, due to high expectations, and too much of glitter.

The role of managers, therefore, must change from that of foul-mouthed, nasty guys to more caring and understanding persons, who can be depended upon. If we want to get the maximum out of people, we must bring creativity into the organisation – we must think with our hearts. We must deal with people, taking into account their emotions, how they feel and react to our remarks. Emotions must become the central point of dealing with our peers, bosses and subordinates. Handle people with care by caring for them.

Battles conceived, directed and fought by the heart are bigger and easier to win as compared to campaigns emanating only out of rationale and logic. Remember, whatever decision you take, affects someone or the other. While looking for human solutions, you can't apply the computer type of logic. Good-hearted people are always liked and respected. Never be nasty to people, because you will most probably be hated for it.

Partiality and prejudice are unfortunately today's global maladies. Class, caste, colour and religion exist today, as much as they did 500 years ago. How may we claim to be a civilised and developed world? Too much prejudice, for too long, generates hatred and is the cause of unrest and terrorism in the world.

'I have never let my schooling interfere with my education.'

– Mark Twain

Partiality and prejudice within organisations, especially based on colour, caste or religion, should never be tolerated. Remember, politics and partiality start from the top. These must be nipped in the bud. If not checked in time, these become killer diseases for the organisation.

The heart and intuition go hand-in-hand. When your heart speaks through intuition – listen to it – it has lot more to say than you can hear. At the end of it all, use your heart to connect with people and try to influence those as well, who are not directly under your control or authority. Let influencing people on the emotional plane become a habit for you.

Be the Best, Whatever You are:

'If you can't be a pine on the top of the hill, be a shrub in the valley – but be the best little shrub by the side of the hills. Be a bush, if you can't be a tree. If you can't be a bush, be a bit of the grass, if you can't be a highway, then just be a trail, if you can't be the sun, be a star; it's not by size that you win or fail – be the best of whatever you are!'

– Douglas Mallock

Your Personal Road Map

1. Promise yourself that you will keep a balance between your heart and your head while taking any decision.

2. Promise yourself that you will show compassion towards people and put yourself in their shoes.

3. Promise yourself that you will leave your worries behind in office when you come back home.

4. Promise yourself that whenever you are in a position of authority, you will not be a pain for people around you.

5. Promise yourself that whenever you are in a position of authority, you will always hold the hand of your subordinates.

6. Promise yourself that you will not show bias or discrimination based on religion, colour or caste.

9

YOUR EMOTIONAL BIO RHYTHM

It is strongly recommended that you do your EQ profiling given on page 271-273 and answer all 20 questions before you look up your Emotional Bio Rhythm (EBR).

Going through the pages of this book you would have realized as to how very complex we human beings are. Our behavior, basic characteristics and our abilities to deal with the world and our environment differ from person to person. These abilities and temperament for each of us is very complex. That is why we also call this complex human behavior as an individual's nature. This implies that these noncognitive aspects of our character are to some extent given to us by nature. That is why there are some who are very cool headed and some of us fly the handle and lose temper at the drop of a hat. These human instincts and basic qualities like will-power, strength of character, etc., make a deep impact on each of us and to a large extent dictates as to how we interpret the world. Each one of us, therefore, has a unique Emotional Bio Rhythm – the way our emotions and characteristics shape our life – which is the key to improving our individual performance.

Emotional Intelligence – as described in the first few chapters – is a mix of an individual's nature, characteristics, traits and attitude. On EI plane we all possess certain strengths as well as weaknesses; most of us have more strengths than weaknesses. To improve upon these weaknesses are like "Emotional Optimization".

To optimize, one must first be able to understand and realize what one possesses – what nature has bestowed upon us. People are born under twelve zodiac signs. These sunsigns are as per English calendar. People born under a particular sunsign possess certain peculiar traits. These can be analyzed and mapped on to the abilities that fall under the domain of Emotional Intelligence.

In *Heart Over Matter,* I have expanded the scope of EI by looking into and integrating EI with aspects like our likes and dislikes, relation between heart and head, our basic emotional structure, passion, determination, motivation, drive, commitment, integrity, principles, mindset and even values.

In a way I have covered the entire domain of human competence which can be labeled as "One's character and Personality". Within our character and personality map, all these qualities are loosely coupled and loosely defined. It is not possible to quantify these traits and represent them as numbers. We call it Emotional Quotient but it would be very difficult to assign a number to one's EQ – at best it would be some sort of an approximation of a very subjective analysis.

Sunsigns define the character and personalities for people born under different sunsigns. Here also the characteristics are loosely defined and loosely structured. It is more of a narrative rather than a grading system. I feel one needs to leave it at that. If these can give us a gross feel about our basic character, we can take that as a starting point in moving towards optimizing our abilities.

Surprisingly these characteristics pretty well match up with things like our sense of humour, delayed gratification, perseverance, optimism, patience, trusting others, impulsive nature, caring for others and so forth.

Sunsigns divides the earth's 6.5 billion population into 12 distinct Zodiac signs. These are considered the twelve basic personality types. People in these groups get their characteristics or personality traits from whatever sign that the sun was passing through at the time of their birth. Since these sunsigns go across a time zone there is an imaginary boundary line between two signs. This imaginary line is called a 'Cusp'. For simple under-standing, people born close to these boundaries tend to have characteristics of both the signs.

As you read your Bio Rhythm as per your sunsign, you

will realize that many of the characteristics match with your character almost 100 per cent. Some of these match to some extent and you would say, "Hm…this could be possible" and some don't match at all and you say, "Oh no! This is not me". But if you take the sum total you will find a number of traits that match yours. Even if it is 80 per cent profile match, it becomes a useful tool. First, you can be conscious about your strengths and weaknesses and second, you can make an effort to bring about a change in yourself. Third you can understand your personality and avoid those situations, jobs and people which do not go along with your personality.

For example, if you are one who cannot work under pressure and tension as per your Emotional Bio Rhythm then you must avoid taking jobs that have an environment or expectation which will have you under pressure.

Your "Self profiling" and Emotional Bio Rhythm put together can give you a fair idea as to how to deal with life, which direction to move into and what type of area of work to choose that goes along well with you.

Therefore you work on two planes together, emotional optimization and optimizing your life according to your temperament. Read on… .

CAPRICORN

Strong willpower, hard work and perseverance are some of the trademarks of a Capricorn. You are therefore able to put in sustained hard work for as long as it takes to achieve your goal. You are very methodical, conscientious willing to take pressures and failures on the way while you are working to accomplish something. You always feel duty-bound to complete the work that has been assigned to you. You are very dependable and stand like a rock in the face of challenges. For an organization you can be an asset. You are mentally tough as steel. On the EQ spectrum these are your strongest points.

You yourself are a perfectionist and expect your subordinates as well as you superior (bosses) to work equally hard. You don't like to take shortcuts, are patient and prepared to wait to get success at any cost. Therefore, most of you demonstrate a high degree of delayed gratification. You make a great manager because of self-discipline; self restraint and sometimes, self-denial, are your basic characteristics. You are like a tortoise who believes in "Slow and steady wins the race". You make a good boss as you appreciate and admire people who are hard working achievers.

You are not a dreamer and approach life cautiously. You don't do star gazing, instead keep your gaze right in front – focused on the target.

You are quite reserved and don't make friends easily. You like to assess a person before letting him in as a friend and therefore have limited number of friends. But you make true friends who are dependable and who can also bank on you. As far as your own looking after is concerned, you avoid seeking help from others and like to do things on your own. On the negative, you are the one who won't forgive easily and may not give people a second chance.

You take great pride in everything that you do and that is why you are very meticulous with your work. You are especially proud of your hard work, and self-denial you can impose on yourself. Because of this people sometimes feel that you have a big ego. You have a high self-esteem and therefore don't take criticism very easily.

As a person, you have tremendous self-confidence and self-belief. You never doubt your abilities and to achieve your goals you can put in sustained hard work. You are shrewd, practical and many times demonstrate that you are unemotional.

Capricorns do possess considerable moral courage and are even prepared to own up one's mistakes, when they feel they have gone wrong. You can raise your voice and thump the table if and when required. You do speak the truth but are cautious enough not to step on others' toes. You handle people pretty well, mind your own business and keep to yourself most of the time.

People of your sunsign have a narrow way of looking at things because you are not very flexible in your approach.

You are more bothered about counting the score rather than enjoying the match. People therefore look at you as stubborn and headstrong. This way, you tend to lose friends and also make some enemies at the end of the day. Learn how to work smart and not only work hard. As a leader you are more into micro-management rather than macro-management. Going higher up in the hierarchy of an organization needs you to delegate work and trust people which unfortunately you don't.

As an individual you are calculative but not impulsive and hate wastage, laziness and even carelessness at all levels. You do not like much of limelight and don't blow your own trumpet. Creativity may not be in your DNA but you beat everybody and compensate this by sheer hard work. You have the ability of bouncing back after a failure. As a team leader you are at times over demanding and want people to be as efficient and hardworking as you are. This makes you look like a heartless person. You have a kind heart and are willing to help those who are in need but outwardly you don't give this impression.

On the whole, you lack initiative and tend to keep a low profile. You are usually guarded in your approach and take initiative only if required. But once you take up a job in hand, you give your best shot and add value to the work on hand. You must make efforts to take credit for your achievements.

You are not after riches and as such not very materialistic in nature. But you are pretty ambitious and are prepared to give your best to achieve what you want. You don't like to take foolish chances, not a gambler by nature instead are very cautious. You are prudent enough to take life realistically rather than choosing to be over-optimistic. To you, world is an unsafe place which rewards only those who are conservative, cautious and hardworking. You are collaborative, at the same time pretty secretive. You can never let your guard down, be released like a child or be spontaneous. At workplace therefore you are a stickler and more often than not you are viewed as a snob.

While taking part in a competition, you appear very ordinary, often even unprepared or ill-equipped but you are a sure winner just because of your hard work, focus and mental tenacity.

YOUR STRENGTHS

- Strong willpower, determination to achieve and perseverance are your strongest points. You have the credo – "When the going gets tough, the tough gets going" – embedded in your DNA. You can accomplish whatever you set out to. So don't hesitate in setting high goals for yourself.

- Self-discipline, being able to set high standards and keeping yourself focused on the target goal is your major asset, and lets you cross the most difficult of the targets.

- You are a highly dependable person, who at times becomes absolutely indispensible for a boss or an organization. People love to have you in their organization. Be aware of this and don't let down people because they expect every bit of sincerity from you.

- You are absolutely sure of yourself and are proud of hard work, determination and even self-denial.

YOUR WEAKNESSES

- Sometimes learn to work smart and not only work hard. Many a time, a shortcut can save effort and time.
- Get rid of the habit of getting into the nitty-gritty of things and look at the larger picture also. As you go higher in the ladder of organizational hierarchy this may become an indispensable part of your work.
- There is a need to be a little flexible as you are pretty rigid about your ideas, convictions and approach.
- You must learn to take initiative. You do not make efforts to start something on your own. If someone takes you to do a job, you do it very well. Remember, a good leader is the one who takes initiative.

FAMOUS CAPRICORN PERSONALITIES

- John Denver
- Richard Nixon
- Mel Gibson
- Isaac Newton
- Joseph Stalin
- Martin Luther King
- Rudyard Kipling
- Mohammad Ali
- Elvis Presley

AQUARIUS

As an individual, you are a very creative person who can think out of the box. That is why people can bank on you for generating new ideas. You are to a large extent intellectual and artistic. You are also a dreamer and sometimes you tend to be impractical as you tend to be looked up in your own ivory tower. At large you are cause-oriented and tend to do things that are good for the society or humanity. You are sensitive to other's needs and hence display a good amount of empathy. You are gentle, humanitarian and many times over-permissive. Being philanthropic by nature, you believe in "Charity begins at home". You tend to be gentle and human and are always prepared to listen to the other side of the story. Aquarians tend to be very emotional and many a time cannot keep control over their emotions. People view you as erratic, sometimes eccentric and in many cases not having a well-balanced mind. You have a high passion quotient and really get involved in something that you like. This nature makes you persuasive to the extent that you tend to become obsessed with a thing. In such cases, it becomes a reason for your getting mentally and physically exhausted which may also injure your health.

You are to a good extent an exhibitionist and sometimes seen as blowing your own trumpet. You make efforts to come into the limelight. Therefore you have that achievement drive in you which pushes you to take initiative. You always have the quest to learn and are more like an explorer. You are rebellious, independent in thinking and refuse to follow the crowd. This nature makes you an inventor in your own right. Many a time you take a more difficult path which you feel is the right one to achieve your goals – however difficult it may be. You display high degree of delayed gratification and can really work hard to achieve what you want to achieve. You are a person of certain principles and are honest as well as loyal to people around you and the organization you work for. You stand up for your rights and those of others and display moral courage. You could be a little moody and even aloof especially when you don't like a thing or an activity and are pretty vocal about it. Since you are an emotional person, you tend to lack self control.

You are not arrogant but many times display a sense of inflated ego. You have an intense desire to communicate with people. You are unfortunately not diplomatic, many times being tactless and rude in your dealing with others. Yet your helpful nature and being "fair to all" attitude makes you a good boss. You have strong likes and dislikes and often take time to choose friends. But once you are sure of a person you become the best of friends. You are not partial and this is viewed as your strength by your friends, your bosses and even your subordinates.

You don't like interference by others and if any suggestions are given to you, these are usually accepted by you at your own terms. At the same time you have high personal ideals and hence demand more from others than is reasonable. If you get deceived you don't forgive or forget easily and you can display your displeasure by outburst of anger. You are very expressive, often humorous, articulate, logical and also have a flair for drama and fine arts.

You display courage to protect those who have been wronged. Since you are viewed as a "well meaning" person, you have good interpersonal skills at an emotional level. You are considerate and believe in fair play for all as well as "collective upliftment". You tend to trust others and many a time can be taken for a ride for this reason.

You are a good listener and are prepared to learn from others and everyone. You are flexible with others to the extent that you can change your opinion if you are convinced that you have been mistaken or when fresh facts come to light.

You are a team player and can perform best in a group. Despite this, you are a leader at heart and would perform better in situations where there is a scope of leading and nobody is breathing down your neck. You need a pep of inspiration to keep going. High on intellect, Aquarians make good teachers or gurus. While working in groups dealing with people you must keep your anger in check and learn to be a little diplomatic.

You are very patriotic and dedicated to the cause. It makes you mature and responsible. You can be relied upon as you are hardworking and industrious. Once you are convinced about something, you can give everything for that cause. You are very supportive for the right things and deeds that you are convinced about. With this backdrop, you are pretty high on the integrity ladder. You are proud of your achievements, and sometimes therefore fear failure. To counter this you tend to become overcautious and even overexuberant, which many people don't like. Sometimes you try to accommodate everyone and tend to be too flexible which could give an impression that you are not sure of what you are doing which actually may not be the case.

YOUR STRENGTHS

- You are proud of your creative abilities and strong convictions. Make efforts to identity your passion and work towards using it to your advantage.

- You can do well in any field because you are open to suggestions. This is your major asset and you must use it to your advantage.

- You care for people in need and therefore are a likeable person. You are helping, understanding, and can make friends easily. This friendly, warm nature can help you create a reliable network of friends.

- You seek to do things your own way and many times take a more difficult path to success. This is a big positive for you as it gives you an innovative edge over others.

YOUR WEAKNESSES

- It is difficult at times for you to control your emotions and this could cloud your decision-making ability.

- Aquarians usually need cheering up and a pep of inspiration to get going. Try to remain self-motivated and don't always wait for compliments.

- You could become overambitious, overexuberant and lose sight of reality. Many a time, you tend to be rather futuristic in your thinking which may lead to failures and frustration.

- You are frank, and being undiplomatic and even rude to people can go against you. You may lose friends and also make some enemies.

FAMOUS AQUARIAN PERSONALITIES

- Charles Dickens
- Abraham Lincoln
- Charles Darwin
- Oprah Winfrey
- General Douglas MacArthur
- Wolfgang Mozart
- Lord Byron
- Franklin D Roosevelt
- Jules Verne
- Eva Braun

PISCES

You are high on social intelligence and quickly gauge what others need. You are always helpful and go all out – even making a personal sacrifice sometimes to help friends and near and dears. This puts you high on Empathy Quotient. You have a cool temperament and nothing upsets or excites you easily. This is liked by others and hence you make a good number of friends. On the flip side you have a sharp tongue, can be very sarcastic and use humour to have fun at other peoples cost. This can break great friendships. Otherwise you are a friend for a lifetime and stand by friends through difficult times as well. You give 100 per cent to your friendship.

You don't lose temper easily. Even if you get angry, you cool down soon. This is a great quality and on the Emotional Intelligence Plane, puts you high on "tolerance". Since you don't brood, you don't let the poison of anger stay in you for very long. Good for you and keep it up. You have a great quality of taking people along, especially those who are weak, downtrodden, or even failures. These are the qualities of a true leader. You are also not very judgmental about the shortcomings of others. Having this quality which helps you become a leader cannot be of much use if you don't take the lead. That, in fact is your great weakness, you lack initiative and have a laidback attitude which becomes a hurdle for your progress. You are neither ambitious, nor competitive and need constant push and encouragement to move on.

You think, "I don't want to be a millionaire but I want to live like one". Remember, you can't have the cake and eat it too. This lack of willpower leads to lack of self-discipline, which makes you lose many opportunities to success. Looking for an easy way out and taking the path of least resistance can lead to a wasted life.

Those of you who can make efforts to swim upstream become Albert Einstein while those who don't make efforts end up doing menial and mediocre jobs all their lives. If you get hold of yourself and just take care of this aspect, your life can really turn around because there is no lack of talent and abilities in you.

Obviously since you lack that pushy aggressive outlook, you want quick results and that too without much efforts. Therefore, you lack a sense of purpose and lack that realization of delayed gratification. You rather prefer instant gratification.

You are a person of high values and impeccable character. You are very trustworthy, highly honest, impartial and are all for "Old fashioned virtues" – which forms a major part of Emotional Intelligence. In that sense you are pretty high on EQ. The best part is that you trust others also and believe in "I trust you till you prove otherwise!"

You are not greedy, but are sensitive about your pride and self-esteem. Obviously, since you are a man of high principles, you don't want people to hurt your pride. You are usually very confident in the areas of your choice. Your confidence is sometimes linked to your mood swing, which is a weak point for you.

You usually want things to remain as they are and therefore like to stay in a protected environment. In this sense you lack moral courage and are not assertive enough. You must learn to speak out and let your opinion be heard. This again is a negative for your leadership acumen. You are pretty adaptable and would adjust to circumstances, places and people quite easily. You are also pretty tuned into everything including feelings of others. You have a sensitive emotional rader, so to say. On the otherside everything appears to be rosy to you and you have an optimistic and positive attitude towards life.

YOUR STRENGTHS

- You can take people along even if they are inferior, weak or even non-performers.
- You have a very positive outlook towards life and view the world through rose colored glasses.
- You are great at making friends and can retain friendship for life. You seldom get angry and your easy-going nature attracts many people towards you.
- You value great values and are an example of a person with high integrity, honesty and fair play.
- You are pretty adaptable to whatever comes in life and take life as it comes. You have no problem in adjusting to people or places.

- You are caring and show great empathy for others. You go for charity and even make personal sacrifice for others.

YOUR WEAKNESSES

- Lack of will power and initiative are your two big weak points. Learn to take initiative, don't be happy with the flow.

- You don't have that sense of delayed gratification. Learn to sacrifice in order to gain something in life. Remember, "No pain, no gain".

- You follow the path of least resistance and lack self-discipline which can make a difference between success and failure for you.

- You lack moral courage and are not assertive about your own opinions.

FAMOUS PISCEAN PERSONALITIES

- Albert Einstein
- Alexander Graham Bell
- Ustad Zakir Hussain
- Aamir Khan
- Elizabeth Taylor
- Bruce Willis
- Mikhail Gorbachev

ARIES

You are very candid about what you want and you make no bones about it. If you want something then you must get it and you don't mind the whole world knowing about it. You tell others what you want even if it is at the cost of irritating them.

At the same time, you as an individual are not cunning or selfish. Your innocence and trusting nature makes you a likeable person. People born under this sunsign are truthful and cannot easily lie. Because of your faith and trust in others, you make a good number of friends, thereby becoming a well-networked individual.

You are emotionally strong and don't let your feelings, especially that of remorse or sadness, surface easily, but you are short on patience. You love to be in the profession that you like and will never be able to give your best in a vocation that does not suit your temperament. You are not subtle, and many times you are very vocal about your dislikes. Therefore you are pretty straightforward and direct – often blunt – in your approach or your remarks. You are usually quick to criticize which at times may annoy people. More often than not, you choose honour and glory over material and money. You love to lead, like a person leads a parade with full pomp and show. Short of patience, you are also short-tempered. Your temper disappears pretty fast and that is good for you.

But your anger is sporadic, unpredictable and could flare up even because of petty things like someone ignoring you. You have a philosophy of "Forgive and forget" and are prepared to say sorry if you feel that you were on the wrong.

Unfortunately you work in "Black and white" mode. To you people are either good or bad and therefore you are a man or woman of strong likes and dislikes. When you move up the ladder in your profession, this can surely be seen as weakness. All those who are not in your good books tend to move away from you. This is bad for your leadership skills. Since you like to lead, this may hamper your progress in general.

In addition you categorize people as either friends or foe. You expect people who are close to you to make it amply clear that they are your close circle at all times. At the same time you can handle all types of people and be comfortable with paupers as well as kings.

Often because of being too interested in your own affairs, people could label you as selfish. You like to look at the bigger picture and usually avoid getting into the nuts and bolts of things. You are very good at social awareness, and know how to deal with different people. You always live in the present and are not much worried about the future. This makes you less worrisome. You are a hardcore optimist about every definable thing. In case faced with adverse circumstances, Aries don't take defeat easily. You can chase success like anything and won't like to take success as a charity. In your pursuit of success, you use more of your brains rather than brawn.

You give a great impression of being sincere and honest. At the same time you would hear what you want to hear. In higher positions many a time you could get encircled by "Coterie" and may not come to know the actual facts. You can bury the past easily and move on. Therefore you are pretty adaptable to people, situations and even new organizations. This also helps you to remain happy as you don't carry additional emotional burden of the past.

Aries would assess a situation quickly and would hate to go into too many details before taking a decision. At the same time, they hate those who are conservative, conformists or are too cautious in their approach.

On the leadership scale you have a joyous nature with a will to achieve. You are a go-getter and can come up with a lots of firsts. Yet you are neither greedy nor a hypocrite. You are not very materialistic, nor do you count your chickens even after they hatch. You may not be a philanthropist, but you are high on the empathy scale and pretty charitable, who would love to see people happy.

YOUR STRENGTHS

- You believe in the motto "Try, try, try again" and are prepared to burn your fingers in the process.
- You have tremendous self-belief and confidence which helps you during times of crisis.
- You are fearless and have a winner's attitude.
- You are neither deceptive nor a cheat or a liar. You look straight in the eye and are firm in your handshake.

- You are a born leader and are like the rocket propellant which gives boost to the rocket engine.
- You are kind-hearted and most of the time generous.

YOUR WEAKNESSES

- Lack of patience along with short-temper can be bad for your personal relations.
- You are moody at times; lack of discipline and lack of responsibility (because sometimes you take things lightly) can be your negatives.
- You are not very flexible, see others in black and white mode or as friends and enemy. This could be a real negative. Therefore you are not high on the adaptability curve.
- You believe in macromanagement and may miss out on details because you don't like to get into the intricacies of a thing.

FAMOUS ARIAN PERSONALITIES

- Marlon Brando
- Charlie Chaplin
- J P Morgan
- Omar Sharif
- Al Gore
- Nikita Khrushchev
- Timothy Dalton
- Julie Christie
- Elton John

TAURUS

You are the one who possess great determination and a strong willpower. Your mental tenacity is as solid as the great rock of Gibralter. You have a stable personality which is not moved by small upheavels of life. You are lucky to be very cool-headed and have a natural gift of a cool temperament. Taurians seldom get annoyed but if they are pushed beyond a point they charge like a bull.

You are neither impulsive nor quick at the draw. As an individual you have tremendous patience and to some extent you are reserved in nature. You are never in a tearing hurry to do things. You seldom worry and are usually confident about yourself and are aware of your strengths. You prefer a peaceful environment which is comfortable and hence prefer status quo. This also makes you more of a home type of a person who would rather prefer friends coming to your place rather than you visiting them. You are not a pessimist but also not a great optimist. You hate change and are very firm about your opinions, beliefs and thoughts. People therefore view you as stubborn and inflexible – which you are. You have certain opinions which are hard to dispel. As a leader or as a manager this becomes an impediment to your progress. You have tremendous emotional strength and are able to sustain emotional burden for a long period without even complaining. This lets you handle today's world and challenges of life without getting any emotional damage.

You are a bit reserved and would prefer to mind your own business and won't go out of the way to make friends. Loyalty to family and friends is your second nature. This makes you a likeable person and therefore people respect you and are fond of you. In addition you are impartial and revenge does not form a part of your vocabulary. You have a generous charitable nature and do reach out to people whenever they need help.

You believe that slow and steady wins the race and score very high on delayed gratification. Therefore you are hardworking, industrious and prepared to put in sustained effort to achieve what you have decided to achieve. You are a very dependable person.

You have a high degree of self-respect and pride. If your pride is hurt, you may forgive a person but it takes a long time for you to forget. You also have tremendous self-confidence and self-belief. You are aware of your strengths and potential to do well in any field. Being stubborn in nature, you are not very adaptable. It is very difficult for people to make you change your decision. In the long run this is a big negative because it is important to be flexible and listen to others if you want to be a successful leader.

You are not very positive about getting new ideas from others or implementing them. You don't like to experiment with new concepts or suggestions. Innovation is not your cup of tea. You are very practical in your approach and hate theoretical discourses or discussions.

You believe in fair play, are considerate and trustworthy.

Since you are reserved people look at you like a person who is aloof. You are also not a good listener because you have your own very strong beliefs. You are not the kind of person who will take the easier path, in fact, you would take the more difficult route to achieve your ambition rather than taking shortcuts. For you everything is backed by hard work. You are not overambitious and are pretty contented by nature.

YOUR STRENGTHS

- Strong willpower, determination and putting in sustained hard work is your major strength.
- You are mentally very strong and can take emotional pressures in your stride.
- Good discipline and being methodical, yet practical is another positive.
- Because you are dependable and reliable, people respect you and come forward to seek your help.

YOUR WEAKNESSES

- Don't overstretch yourself. You tend to do this because you are aware of your tenacity and strength.
- You are very rigid and stubborn. Learn to be flexible and listen to others.
- You can't handle change easily. In today's world where change is the only constant, you may find it difficult to manage your affairs.
- Sometimes you can take a hurt straight to your heart and keep worrying about it for a long time.

FAMOUS TAURIAN PERSONALITIES

- Sachin Tendulkar
- Harry S Truman
- Madhuri Dixit
- William Shakespeare
- Jack Nicholson
- Florence Nightingale
- Leonardo Da Vinci
- Rabindra Nath Tagore
- Andre Agassi
- Al Pacino

GEMINI

You love to live a life which is full of fun, devoid of labour and hard work. You get bored with routine and would love to have new things, situations and jobs. You are fickle-minded, and poor at decision-making. You also waver from decisions made by you earlier and your colleagues think that you don't stand by your decisions or opinions. You are not very tough mentally and therefore do not have a strong willpower. You like multitasking but are not very good at prioritizing the tasks that you undertake. This shortcoming coupled with a wavering mind leads you to various dilemmas or at least dilemma like situations. Therefore, you are neither focused nor consistent in your methods.

You are a rolling stone that gathers no moss. Therefore, you don't stick to the jobs or plans that you make. Impatient to get results, you are usually restless and would score a low on delayed gratification. You are otherwise disciplined, practical and quite organized. But because you have a wavering attitude your work gets delayed.

Your ability to handle multiple tasks at the same time makes you a good manager where such situations arise almost on a day-to-day basis. You are clever, possess a great wit and intellectual abilities which can spell success for you in any field that you choose. You are an innovator who can think out of the box. You are a little moody and this can be offensive for your friends and colleagues.

An honest person, you are a dependable friend to have. You also have a big self-esteem and are proud of yourself. To get your pride back you can be revengeful and will go out of your way to settle the scores. So much so that you can attack from the rear to take your revenge. Being a good communicator you can win any argument by articulating and protecting your point of view in a very effective manner to the audience. You are good at making friends and get along well with others easily. Your self-esteem can sometime lead you to be egoistic.

It's a god's gift that you are very versatile and pretty self-confident. You can take up challenges in life. Adaptability and handling different situations is your big positive trait. Many times you rush like mad to achieve your goals and miss many good things of life. You have a helping nature and love to involve yourself in social work. You have a strong conscience and therefore speak out loud and clear against people and situations which you feel are not right. You can be a whistleblower and are prepared to thump the table if you discover that something wrong is being done. You fight for yourself and the cause that you undertake. Many a time, your friendships are based on your ideology and you can break up a friendship, if there is a mismatch of thinking on moral terms. You, therefore, have an ethical approach towards problems and moral courage is a part of your being. You can dig your heels against people and even your bosses for certain things that you think are wrong.

You are like a chameleon who can adapt to the environment very quickly. Therefore folks like you are very adaptable. You can also keep a straight face in any situation or any adverse circumstances. You can see both sides of the coin and therefore are in a better position to take a realistic decision.

Although you grasp new ideas and plans easily, you are not very consistent in implementation. In that you can leave an assignment halfway through. You are like a restless child who gets tired of a new toy in a few days and looks for another one.

You think young and think positive. This keeps you mentally active and pretty buoyant. Your interests keep changing and you love to abandon old things and start afresh to experiment with something new. You look at the world as one big village and strongly believe that people support each other. As long as an activity doesn't effect your own comforts and well-being, you can go out of the way to help people. You have that empathy in you which compels you to help others, who are less fortunate. Generally, you are affectionate and generous with the people whom you deal with.

You thrive on intellectual discussions and gossip. This makes you a nice and a welcome friend by most people. You can never be a boring company, and are good on the social circuit. You have a good memory for jokes and anecdotes which you can dole out in good measures at parties and get-togethers. People who can match up your mental prowess can be your lifetime friends and you can be a great friend and are very good at networking.

YOUR STRENGTHS

- You have the ability to solve riddles and can look at both sides of the coin.
- You are an innovator and a thinker who can come up with true new ideas.
- A born communicator you are full of wit and charm.
- You can make friends easily and are good at networking with people.
- You can handle multiple tasks without getting worried or stressed.
- You have a high self-esteem.
- You are very adaptable and can handle change very well.
- You have strong courage of conviction and can speak out against any wrong being committed.

YOUR WEAKNESSES

- Your big ego can go against you and this may end up breaking relationships.
- You are restless and cannot remain on a task or assignment for too long.
- You can handle a number of tasks but cannot prioritize them.
- You want quick results and are at many times, impatient.
- You cannot remain focused on something for long.
- You are fickle-minded and cannot stick to your opinions and ideas.

- You are revengeful if your ego is hurt.
- You need an outside support to keep up your positive outlook.
- You have a forgiving attitude and people can take advantage of you.

FAMOUS GEMINIAN PERSONALITIES

- Ian Fleming
- John F Kennedy
- Angelina Jolie
- Clint Eastwood
- Johnny Depp
- Marilyn Monroe
- Queen Victoria
- Paul Mc Cartney
- Robert Ludlum
- Salman Rushdie
- Steve Waugh
- Dean Martin
- Morgan Freeman

CANCER

You are a family-oriented person who would like to stick to your roots. You prefer peace and harmony at home. You are traditional and love to celebrate festivals and religious activities in and around your family. At the same time, you love your country and are a deep-rooted patriotic person.

Helping others, grooming those who need it is your second nature. You help others even materially as well as monetarily. Yet your emotions are concealed behind your tough exterior. People don't find it easy to understand you and if hurt by someone you withdraw into a shell. You would perform well if your family life is healthy and happy. While dealing with others, you hold remarks in your head for too long – holding on to every word that has been said. For the outside world you appear to be unemotional, shrewd, stubborn and even thick skinned. But to your near and dear ones you are gentle, kind and sensitive. You are an introvert but yet not averse to socializing. Cancerians appreciate art, literature and other fine arts and many of them possess artistic prowess in a reasonable measure.

You fantasize relationships and are often seen as romantic and emotional. But with your spouse and children, you are loyal and very protective. You are also a loyal and dependable friend. You can give a lot to others without expecting anything from them. You have very strong memories of your childhood which you can easily recall – many times even driven by them.

In your day-to-day affairs and dealings you are neither very organized nor meticulous. You brood over insults for a long-time and cannot take a negative feeling out of your system very easily or even quickly. You many time display a behavior which indicates that you are not very stable with your occupation. You tend to change jobs and display instability in your career path. But you are confident about yourself and can withstand pressure.

You can be oversensitive and are hurt by imaginary hurts – causes which actually don't exist. You can't obey orders easily, getting upset if someone orders you to do a job. You are not a conformist at that and this can hamper your chances of good jobs. You also tend to fall for flattery and also tend to change your opinions. If you are ticked off too often by your bosses, you would even think seriously of resigning. Cancerians should always look at those people who manage their jobs as well as bosses well. If you keep a low profile, not speaking out too often, you can very well outperform others. In general, you are not a very likeable person by the bosses as well as collegues, but those of who learn this art of getting along well can really do well in life. As far as work is concerned, you are very dependable and have a very high personal integrity. You are also a reliable friend. Procrastination is a part of your behavior and you tend to put off things until the last minute which usually upsets those who value time.

If your mood is good you can motivate others but if it is not upbeat you could become a big demoraliser. Your empathy factor is high because you not only understand other people's pain but have the ability to even "feel it". In general you are very protective about your friends and family. You are emotionally attached to your past and love to preserve old things like letters, photographs or even things from schools.

People outwardly see you as a person who lacks initiative and drive. In fact, you work in a low key manner and prefer to maintain a low profile. Yet you create a workplace full of cooperation, harmony and happiness. You are a true leader and can lead people even if you don't have authority over them. You have a strong will-power and self-control. You are high on delayed gratification and are prepared to put in what it takes to achieve your goal. Even if you encounter failure, you can bounce back after that. Since you are not a show off, your efforts may go unnoticed sometimes but your efforts must be recognized as you love to be appreciated.

You are little rigid about your ideas and not very flexible in your approach.

YOUR STRENGTHS

- A strong willpower and ability to work under pressure are your two major strengths.
- You are protective about others and have the ability to feel the need and pain of others.
- You have a high level of confidence and take pride in what you do.
- You are a true leader and can motivate others to achieve their goals. You have a positive attitude.

YOUR WEAKNESSES

- You are not very adaptable; learn to be a little flexible.

- You can't take insult very easily and at times can't even take a remark against you.

- You postpone things to the last minute and are not in any hurry to finish the task at hand.

- You must control your mood swings – these can hamper your work and your productivity.

FAMOUS CANCERIAN PERSONALITIES

- John Rockfeller
- Julius Ceaser
- Princess Diana
- Helen Keller
- Tom Hanks
- Tom Cruise
- Harrison Ford
- Pamela Anderson
- Meryl Streep
- Giorgio Armani
- Nelson Mandela
- George Bush
- Mike Tyson

LEO

You are strong willed, courageous and ambitious. In your approach towards life you are very positive and are straightforward in your dealings. You are a level headed person and have an uncomplicated personality.

Many of you think you are born to lead and most of you are. You have the ability to attract people towards you and are able to build and even to an extent manipulate public opinion to your advantage. You are also ambitious and therefore prefer to take charge of people as well as a situation. You like to hog the limelight and are always open to flattery. To boss around is in your blood. You are well-disciplined and also expect others to be disciplined and responsive.

You are to an extent stubborn – specially about your beliefs – and lack that flexibility which good leaders must have. You must learn to bend rules but need not break them.

Arrogance can come in the way of great leaders and arrogant you are. You display haughtiness and wear autocratic pride on your sleeve. You are at times arrogant and conceited. As a leader you are a good organizer, courageous and tend to be chivalrous at times. You think big and also have a speculative nature. You love doing things big. You are tough-headed and have a strong will-power. You like to be independent.

On the flip side if you are a good leader, you don't cooperate and take orders easily. You also trust your close ones blindly and are often disappointed as people can't live up to your expectations. You are also not very good at judging people and their intentions.

As an individual you are sensitive to personal criticism and can go into a fit of rage if your leadership or ideas are questioned. You also love to be the centre of attraction and want people to praise you. You also have that greed for power more than greed for money or material.

You dislike petty mindedness and love pomp and show as well as grandeur. You like to live life king size – whether you are a king or not. You like to live on the edge and dislike drudgery and day-to-day living.

You cannot take personal criticism easily. In fact your ego is pretty bloated all the time and because of that you are very sensitive about your own image. If you are criticized, then at times you may decide to leave a job in the middle of it. This can be a negative because people start thinking that you are not dependable. You are patient and are willing to put in efforts to get results. Given a choice, you would take the tougher and the right path rather than taking a short cut. In the same spirit, you don't allow your subordinates to take shortcuts. You like to meet deadlines and finish your work well in time. You are punctual and meticulous. Because of your positive attitude you always want things to go your way and when things do not happen that way you lose your composure and react immediately.

Your team as well as organization can bank on you as you are pretty dependable. Since you are ambitious, you tend to bite more than what you can actually chew. Therefore, you always have a lot on your plate. At the same time, you don't do things which you are not convinced about. You are pretty moralistic and have your own code of conduct which you rigidly impose on yourself as well as others. You don't bend rules for yourself or even for others – even for your closest friends and family. You are generous to others and believe in forgiving and forgetting. It is good because you don't brood over things and don't ever keep grudges to your heart. It is good for you because you don't keep that excess emotional baggage in your system for too long. People can depend on you and usually you don't ask for anything in return. You are also an extrovert and have lot of friends. It is true because people are attracted towards you. Since you are outgoing, honest and straightforward it is easy for you to make friends and also retain them. Sometimes your temper can get into your relationships. In addition you want to have the last word in every situation or argument. This is not a very good quality for people who want to be socially upward mobile. Because of this you may lose some friends and your popularity may take a beating.

YOUR STRENGTHS

- You are patient and are prepared to work hard and want to achieve your goals.
- Self-discipline and imposing the same discipline for your team also is a strong positive trait that you possess.

- You are a born leader and people naturally tend to follow you. You can turn the tide in your favour by influencing other people positively.

- You have a positive attitude and also a streak of bravado – these can be of immense use during times of crisis.

- You easily forgive and forget and don't keep things to your heart. You move on with life and don't brood over small things.

- You are broad-minded, think big, like to live and do things king size.

YOUR WEAKNESSES

- Your ego and attitude as well as autocratic pride can make you unpopular. You must try to remain grounded and realistic.

- You are all the time in the lead and therefore not a good follower. Remember, a good leader should also learn to be led.

- Sometimes you think bigger than what can be achieved. You bite more than what you can chew.

- You expect everyone to be fair and not to use any unfair means. Sometimes in the practical world this does not happen.

- You are stubborn and don't move an inch from your ethos and belief. You may not break the rule but at times you can bend it.

- You trust near ones blindly. This must be guarded against.
- You have that greed for power and flattery.

FAMOUS LEO PERSONALITIES

- Napoleon Bonaparte
- Henry Ford
- Fidel Castro
- Benito Mussolini
- Barack Obama
- George Bernard Shaw
- General Norman Schwarzkopf
- Arnold Schwarzenegger
- J K Rowling
- Robert Redford
- Bill Clinton
- Neil Armstrong
- Danielle Steel
- Jackie Kennedy

VIRGO

You are conservative, fastidious, laborious and tend to look at everything in life very critically. You are happy with things as they are and are not the adventurous kind who can follow their passion. But lack of passion is compensated by your exactness and being meticulous for everything that you do. You are at times very myopic in your approach and rather take a micro-view than a macro-view of things. Therefore most Virgos are tacticians and not strategists. This comes in their way becoming great leaders.

You are very judicious, impartial and display considerable charm, dignity and panache while dealing with people. Not very outgoing, you end up making few friends. You do not trust others and are unable to trust your own abilities and judgment. In this way you can become indecisive at times. In addition you feel that nobody can do a job better than you.

Thoroughness and an eye for detail is your hallmark. When looking at things in general, you always end up finding a mistake or two. You are clearheaded and can simplify the most complicated problems. You are cool and calm and do not lose temper easily. You usually keep a low profile and don't blow your own trumpet. At the same time you are pretty egoistic.

You feel that hard work is a good way of winning hearts.

You can seldom display emotions and not easily express love as it is usually done. You can be trusted with work and your employer or boss will always be happy with your work which you carry out perfectly. You give importance to be neat and clean and pay particular attention to good order and discipline. Your desk is usually pretty clean and you expect the same from others as well. Since you are very precise in viewing and analyzing things, you tend to miss out the larger picture.

Sometimes being over careful can get the better of you and you tend to get worried in those situations which are not that difficult to handle. You end up making a mountain out of a molehill in many of your endeavors. As a boss you are demanding and expect an exacting performance from your subordinates. You are unable to tolerate shabby work or a half-hearted effort by others.

You feel that to be loveable or likeable you need to be a perfectionist. You do create a good work ethics around you. You are not the emotional type and do not wish to display emotions, hence people misconstrue you as emotionally insensitive or even crippled.

You are self-motivated and would like to take on work on practical problems rather than theoretical ones. Practical problems excite you. You are meticulous but not spontaneous in nature. You always strive to improve things, the environment, the people and everything in general. Value addition is in your blood and your people can bank on it. Some of you try to remain aloof and don't make efforts to come into the limelight.

A fairly independent personality, you always feel that you do not require anybody else's assistance or help in doing your work. Your credo is "Perfect has to be good", or alternatively, "If you are good, you got to be perfect". This leads to your being very flawless in life. You have a good sense of self-esteem and pride; are honest in your dealings, but not easily adaptable. Virgos are neither highly creative nor very artistically inclined but are very thorough and do take life pretty seriously. You do care for others but won't go out of your way to help people at large. You are not showoffs and try to mind your own business. Your attitude is aristocratic, reserved and precise. Not very materialistic, you are careful with your money.

YOUR STRENGTHS

- Taking huge amount of pain, making efforts sincerely to finish the job at hand and being meticulous makes you an indispensable person for the organization you work for. You have good willpower and have tremendous patience.

- You are generous to others who are genuinely in need. You let your heart rule your head. You are happiest when you are solving problems for others.

- You love to be organized and keep your surroundings absolutely neat and clean. This gives you an edge over others.

YOUR WEAKNESSES

- You don't trust people and sometimes you don't trust even yourself. This leads to lack of self-confidence and may hamper your friendship circle.

- You not only micro-manage things but also view things in too much of detail. This may lead to your missing out the main issue or major aspects of life.

- You do not want too many changes to happen in life, in work and in general. This gives an impression that you lack initiative and drive.

- You are a good critic but you are yourself not perfect. You are always bothered about improvement and refinement. This can slow down your overall progress and success.

FAMOUS VIRGOAN PERSONALITIES

- Sophia Loren
- Leo Tolstoy
- Queen Elizabeth
- Mother Teresa
- Yasser Arafat
- Michael Jackson
- Sean Connery
- Lyndon Johnson
- Agatha Christie

LIBRA

People love to interact and befriend you because you have a very pleasant personality. You hate to be rude and love to be a mediator and patch up quarrels and fights between others. You are an extrovert as well as a good listener. You have that great ability to understand other person's point of view. In this lies the great art and charm of diplomacy – which you are very good at. People come to you to share their personal problems and always find you to be warm and accommodating. You like to make everyone happy and love peace and harmony for which you can sacrifice anything. You are ready to bend down and compromise in order to maintain peace with everyone. You hate bloodshed and tensions. You are good at and prefer planning and strategizing rather than execution where you may have to face problems and even dirty your hands. In war – if you are in it – you would rather be a general who would plan the battle and hate to be actually fighting on the front line. You like status quo and wouldn't like your life to have any kind of turbulence. Your empathy quotient is pretty high and you can actually feel the pain of others, therefore you would say that 'I feel your agony' rather than saying 'I understand your agony' to those who are going through a problem. You have that indecisive nature which shows you in poor light. Indecisiveness is caused by fear of failure.

You do not have a strong willpower and are not mentally very tough. You cannot work under too much pressure and also prefer to live a good, happy life of luxury. You lack consistency in hard work and usually work in fits and starts. It is difficult for you to perform and put in hard work over a prolonged period of time. If a task has to be done, you tend to slow down after the initial enthusiasm subsides. When you get tired, you need a long period to rest and get refit. You do get your energies in spurts and go through low and high phases of energy. You also go, ding-dong on the emotional plane as well; at points in time you are calm, charming and happy and many times you could just be the opposite. But more often than not, you can keep a check on your anger being displayed on your face. You are a good planner because you can take a 360 degree view of things. You consider all aspects, weigh out pros and cons before you take a call.

You are not very ambitious and are contented with what you have. This is a big boon as in today's world everybody is very ambitious and greedy. In a way you have a laid back attitude – never in a hurry to do lots of things together. You have enough patience and are high on delayed gratification. You are grateful for what you have. If everything runs smoothly and nobody bothers you, it is the happiest situation for you.

You are very honest but can buckle under undue pressure. Even your integrity may be questioned if you come under pressure because you may commit something which is against the morals of the society.

You have a flexible nature. Main reason for this is that you do not dig heels against anybody or any situation. You let the storm pass by rather than getting caught in the storm. Therefore you are good at maintaining peace at work and at home. You are good at managing other people on the emotional plane and hence can manage them well. You can praise people more than what they actually deserve. Therefore managing bosses is easy for you. This way, even if you are not ambitious as well as hard working, you tend to climb the professional ladder. But you can be easily taken for a ride and many times people take advantage of this.

You don't take undue initiative. You need to be jump started and therefore need a push to get into a venture. Yet you are optimistic and have a positive frame of mind. You have that knack of achieving things through peaceful means. You always project a down-to-earth image and to an extent you are.

YOUR STRENGTHS

- You are a great mediator and are very good at conflict resolution.
- Pleasant personality and a friendly nature.
- High on empathy and having the ability to connect with everyone and feel their pain.
- Boss management and handling people at emotional level.
- You have a laid back, unambitious attitude. This is a big positive in today's dog eat dog world. Most of

the people around us are not happy with what they have.

- You are a dependable friend.
- Keeping everyone happy. At least you make all out efforts to keep peace at home and workplace.

YOUR WEAKNESSES

- Your overindulgence and getting into excessive mode of some kind or the other. Overeating, excessive use of alcohol are some examples.
- Not taking initiative and working in fits and starts.
- You love life of luxury and are not disciplined.
- Unable to take pressure.
- Not having a firm opinion of yours about situations and issues. You don't speak up against any wrong being done to you or others. In a way you lack moral courage.
- Flip-flop decision/opinion making. You can have some opinion today and suddenly change it the other day.

FAMOUS LIBRAN PERSONALITIES

- Alvin Tofler
- Alfred Nobel
- Cliff Richard
- Eleanor Roosevelt
- Jimmy Carter

- John Lennon
- Lee Iacocca
- Mahatma Gandhi
- Margaret Thatcher
- Mario Puzo
- Oscar Wilde
- P G Wodehouse
- Ray Kroc

SCORPIO

You know what you are and are pretty aware of your strengths and weaknesses. You cannot be influenced by others to change your own opinion about yourself. You are also not easily won over by flattery.

You have an emotional mastery to the extent that external factors do not easily effect your facial expression, as if wearing a mask to hide your emotions. So you do not let the emotions show on your face. You may have a boiling inner nature but you are able to display outward calm. You do not smile often but whenever you do, it is genuine.

In a similar way your body language also doesn't give away joy or sorrow or even nervousness. Neither do you show your pride nor display your dismay or shock. You have an overall asset that you don't react to things easily. This helps you in handling life which is a roller coaster of emotional ups and downs.

You can judge others (also their intentions) but won't allow others to judge you. People in this respect need to be very careful of you. You have a perfect disguise and can fool others easily about your intentions. You may do a happy talk and look soft but are really tough inside.

Dealing with people is not easy for you for the simple reason that you are not diplomatic. Instead, you are blunt and absolutely frank while passing your opinions about others. You don't bother if the other person is sensitive or care about his feelings. This puts you very high on the moral courage continuum, but gets you many enemies. Please remember, being transparent does not mean being naked! This trait is linked to your self-esteem and you score pretty high on that. You don't show-off your pride but are conscious of your strengths and your self-respect, all the time.

Flattering others is not your cup of tea. But whenever you praise any one, it is a genuine praise. You make either great friends or arch enemies. You are very loyal to your friends. You are also high on empathy for people who are sick or are in need of help. You have awesome inner strength and you can really use it to your advantage. You also have strength to face pain, poverty, deprivation and even defeat and are ready to take any blow as well as ever prepared to come out of it.

You repay people who have helped you or who have been kind to you. But in case of an insult, you hit back very hard to completely hurt the person. You sometimes are so ruthless in hitting back that you demolish or destroy the other person completely. In some ways you are very revengeful. You have a very strong willpower and are mentally tough. You are self-motivated and have strong determination and a job given to you is usually considered done – you don't know the word quit and don't easily give up once you have accepted an assignment. At the same time, you tend to be a loner and lack the ability to work in a team. You have the spirit of 'Never say die'. You can therefore do very well and reach the top of any profession because of your hardwork.

Bouncing back after a setback is not difficult for you. If your intention is to achieve something, you can go for it all out and achieve it. Nothing is impossible for you. You are very possessive of what you feel is yours; this could be materialistic stuff or even success.

You are very strong about your opinions – to the extent of being rigid. You don't like things or situations which are not in line with your comfort level.

You plan a lot and wait for the right moment to actually act. At the same time you are very hardworking and work for long hours. Packing your day with series of jobs in hand, you love competition at work as well as games and sports. You are tough, determined and strong, and display a positive attitude.

YOUR STRENGTHS

- You have a strong willpower and are mentally tough.
- You know your strengths and weaknesses. This is a huge asset.
- You can bounce back after a failure.
- You can put in real hard works to get your results. You are prepared to wait for success and don't expect results overnight.
- You don't jump or fall flat if something goes wrong and have good control on your emotions.
- You have a soft corner for the deprived people, and are high on empathy.

YOUR WEAKNESSES

- It is difficult for you to commit to a cause. You need to be persuaded to accept a challenge or a concept.
- You are not a team player and want to achieve things alone.
- You can be quite revengeful. You can be very rude to others because of your big ego.
- You are not diplomatic and in simple words, very blunt.

FAMOUS SCORPIAN PERSONALITIES

- Pablo Picasso
- Bill Gates
- Prince Charles
- Indira Gandhi
- Theodore Roosevelt
- Richard Burton
- Charles De Gaulle
- Madame Curie
- Aishwarya Rai
- Bryan Adams
- Jack Welch
- Jawahar Lal Nehru
- Julia Roberts
- Peter Drucker

SAGITTARIUS

Sagittarians are happy go lucky and don't seem to take life seriously. Your motto is "Take life as it comes". You are aware of the fact that luck usually favours you and hence you love taking risks and chances all throughout your life. You are also high spirited and blessed with a high happiness quotient. By nature you love danger and being on the edge, whether it is sports, work or life in general. Speed, fast cars and even roller coaster rides attract you like a bee is attracted to honey.

You are not a conformist and would best perform when your bosses don't breath down your neck. You seldom ask for help or assistance and would rather perform and finish a task alone. You are also a rebel against authority and rules. You love to break rules by nature.

You have good amount of resistance and have the fighter in you. Life and upheavels can rarely beat or defeat you permanently. Sickness doesn't keep you down for long and in that sense you are pretty strong. Risk taking is in your blood and therefore you are a gambler by nature but you are most of the time able to control that urge to speculate.

While dealing with people you are kind-hearted, and willing to share a meal and even lend money to those who ask – sometimes not even bothering to get the money back. At the same time you have a violent temper and can be sarcastic with people. Although romantic in nature you take your time to get permanently settled with someone. You are friendly, cool natured and can network well with people, but sometimes your temper and sarcasm may become a stumbling block in the way to making friends, and especially retaining them.

The positive is that after a fiery display of temper, you tend to feel remorse and are ready to make amends. You may hurt someone today but would present a bouquet of flowers to the person the next day. You are very good-hearted and never keep things in your heart for long. In a way it is good for you as you are not burdened too much with any guilt as such.

You are very caring and empathetic towards those who need help. You could, for example, adopt a stray animal or help those who have been rendered homeless. You won't mind some distant cousin or an old friend staying with you for a couple of months and you would take good care of him with generous hospitality – expecting nothing in return. Travelling and meeting people is what you love. This gives you opportunity to make new friends and chances to figure out new avenues for progress.

You have a very positive attitude and believe that tomorrow will be better than yesterday and today is pretty good and interesting. You are optimistic about everything, have a good imaginative mind and are progressive in thinking. You would, therefore, act first and consider the consequences later. Due to your carefree nature you could become careless at times and this is reflected by your misplacing personal belongings like pens, wallets and umbrellas. You do have a good memory for remembering dates, events and even details of books, etc., but seldom keep grudges against others and believe in "Life is too short to be worried about small things."

You may not be totally honest but you can't easily lie and get caught even if you try it. Since you are comfortable with taking risks and chances, you are usually fearless which helps you achieve a lot in your life.

You do have a great sense of pride, self-esteem and self-worth. Most of you seek the spotlight and want people to appreciate you and your work. Acting, stage and show business attracts you.

YOUR STRENGTHS

- Of a happy go lucky disposition, you are easy to get along with.

- You have a positive attitude towards life. Life seldom defeats you permanently.

- You never run away from a fight and are courageous in every situation.

- You like to manage things on your own and rarely ask for help. You are therefore very dependable. You have tremendous confidence and never hesitate while approaching an assignment. You are very much self-assured.

- Since you are adventurous by nature, you get into new and even risky ventures without hesitation.

YOUR WEAKNESSES

- You sometimes think bigger than what you should. There is a need for you to be a little more practical. Don't depend too much on luck.

- You are not very serious about life and therefore may take certain major decision without weighing out all the options. Guard against this.

- You are weak on delayed gratification because the gambler in you wants quick results by luck or by chance.

- You don't respect authority and are a rebel in that sense. Everything cannot go our way every time and this could harm your interest in certain situations.

- You are too frank about your opinions. Learn to be a little diplomatic.

FAMOUS SAGITTARIAN PERSONALITIES

- Winston Churchill
- John F Kennedy
- Steven Spielberg
- Mark Twain
- Bruce Lee
- Monica Seles
- Brad Pitt
- Osho, Bhagwan Rajneesh

Epilogue

*'Men occasionally stumble over the truth, but
most of them pick themselves up and hurry as
if nothing ever happened.'*

— Winston Churchill

The new millennium has arrived and so have our problems.
The ailments of today's affluent society are not only
limited to our physical being, they are also related to the
deficiencies at the emotional level. There will be more
sickness in the mind than in the body.

Westernisation, media exposure, availability of goods and
materialistic comforts combined with peer pressure, the
breakdown of family structures and spending lesser time
with one's parents is playing havoc with our lives.

The new generation is in a hurry for success, leading to
job-hopping and cut-throat competition, which makes

people self-centered, often disconnected with their peers, insensitive to subordinates and critical of their bosses. The new breed couldn't care less for the companies they work for, or the family members who they live with. Brotherhood, family bonds, patriotism, sacrifice and attachment are becoming old-fashioned concepts. We are making a global village with everything else, but a heart.

As a result, our workforce is less emotionally intelligent, is insensitive and selfish. This is the new corporate India. This phenomenon has already been experienced by developed countries and is now rapidly invading the developing world.

> *'Nowadays people know the price of everything and the value of nothing.'*
>
> – Oscar Wilde

Developing countries, especially the ones in Asia that have a legacy of strong, rich cultures, and deep-rooted human values at their very cores, should leverage their heritage.

They should imbibe good things from the West, like professionalism, respect for time, professional honesty, hard work and being perfectionists, but should cleverly preserve the good aspects of their culture. A good mix of these strong values and professionalism as demonstrated by the West, would usher in progress without degenerating our minds.

We need to build good people and good organisations. Brick and mortar alone, doesn't build organisations. Strong firms are made of good people who are good human beings, people who care for each other and those who care for the organisations they belong to.

This cannot be achieved by steep pay packages alone, or providing attractive e-sops. We will have to move beyond providing swanky offices, well-equipped gyms and well-stocked cafeterias. All good organisations have tried these methods, but very few of them would have succeeded in earning employees' loyalty in the real sense. To earn someone's time, these materialistic sops may be adequate, but in order to earn someone's loyalty and commitment, we will have to move into the emotional domain.

Investing in a strong organisational culture, which is rooted in basic human values, is going to be the *mantra* for survival as well as excellence. Building trust, caring for each other and 'demonstrating' at the highest level of leadership that we value strong human commitments, should be the strategy adopted by the top leadership if they want to build organisations that will last the storm. Stop worrying so much about professional skill sets, technical knowledge or managerial acumen. Work on and give adequate weightage to those basic human traits, that are the must-have skills. Remember, a 10 per cent less competent engineer should be acceptable, but a 10 per cent less human being would never do.

Leaders must understand the hidden levers that move people and drive organisations. Processes, procedures and policies can be easily copied, certifications can be obtained, but cultures have to be created and cultivated. Organisations that build strong cultures would have automatically patented themselves because it is not easy to copy these things. Such organisations will always distinctly stand apart from others and would be able to nurture excellence through their value systems. Armed forces across the world have strong 'traditions', unwritten laws and well-practiced codes of conduct. These have stood the test of turbulent times. That is why, the sense of camaraderie, belonging and the spirit to sacrifice is so strong in the men and women in uniform. These are the signs of strong organisations.

'You never know what is enough, unless you know what is more than enough.'

– Tao

You can't transform people as they enter the workplace. We need to work on them when they are much younger. **We need to make schools a place where kids are taught to be more emotionally intelligent, equipped with social skills and golden hearts.** Emotionally sensitive children will also do well in their respective academic areas. School teachers will have to project themselves in a better manner by demonstrating high moral values, so that they are emulated and respected by the students.

Parents have a great role to play in this 'neo affluent' society. They have to find time for their children to teach them the basic habits of patience, perseverance, respecting others, respecting what is right and most of all, building self-esteem and self-respect. Instead of taking short-cuts and the patronage of parents and the 'parental clout', let them learn to fend for themselves to taste their own sense of achievement. Unfortunately, this is not what is being done. Parents have become over-protective, often encouraging their children to take short-cuts to success, disregarding the law and often showing off their might with whatever little or more they have.

Unfortunately, the value system has eroded steadily over the last 50 years across all fronts. We need to work at all levels to restore it – in organisations, schools as well as at home.

As individuals, we need to work on ourselves and that may be the biggest contribution that we would make to save the situation. The change must start from within. Take care of yourself and the rest will follow. Values and goodness apart, it is also important to live your life in a way, which would satisfy you.

Life is like an egg – and you get only one egg. You decide whether you make an omelette out of it, a scrambled egg, a full-boiled, a half-boiled or a single fry. Sunny side up, that's the way I like it – its your life and you have to live it.

It's worth going back in time and looking back on what you did, what thrilled you and what you enjoyed. Also, ponder over what you didn't like and yet did it because everybody did so, or someone told you to do it. Learn from the past, the mistakes you made for which you would say, 'I wish I did' or 'I wish I didn't.' Make it happen now and don't make the same mistakes that you made in the past. It will be gratifying.

'Be not ashamed of mistakes and thus make them crimes.'

– Confucius

If you have been pushing yourself too hard, ask yourself, 'for what?' It doesn't mean that we take a laid-back attitude towards life and stop working. All that I am saying is, that one must understand the difference between hard work and pushing oneself too hard. There is a thin, dividing line between the two, but everyone must make an effort to find that line and live a balanced life. This way, you will live a better life as a professional, as a citizen, as a member of a family and as an individual.

Live life innovatively. Creativity is about thinking out of the box, breaking mundane rules and abandoning the routine, which everybody follows. It is about trying out something, which no one else has tried. Use creativity to live a richer life, which satisfies you. Remember, creativity is not only restricted to painting or writing poetry. How you handle different people is creativity. Handling various situations better than others is creativity. Handling a conflict is creativity. Handling yourself in a better manner and handling life as it comes, is creativity.

So, use the genius, that we all have, to live life in a more meaningful manner so that at the end of the day, you have no regrets.

The best prayer for any track event

' Oh Lord, in this glorious sport, I pray that you will let me run well. Help each man running against me to do his best, too. Go along with each of us.'

Plan to make a personal change.

Having read all about human instincts and strengths by now, make an honest attempt to profile yourself on the following parameters.

How do you rate yourself on a scale of 10 for the following? (10 being the best and 1 being the worst).

1. Making friends

1 2 3 4 5 6 7 8 9 10

2. Caring for others

1 2 3 4 5 6 7 8 9 10

3. Impulse control

1 2 3 4 5 6 7 8 9 10

4. Getting out of a bad mood

1 2 3 4 5 6 7 8 9 10

5. Anger Management

1 2 3 4 5 6 7 8 9 10

6. Your self-motivation level

1 2 3 4 5 6 7 8 9 10

7. Patience

1   2   3   4   5   6   7   8   9   10

8. Optimism

1   2   3   4   5   6   7   8   9   10

9. Taking criticism positively

1   2   3   4   5   6   7   8   9   10

10. Sense of Humour

1   2   3   4   5   6   7   8   9   10

11. Compassion

1   2   3   4   5   6   7   8   9   10

12. Delayed gratification

1   2   3   4   5   6   7   8   9   10

13. Attitude

1   2   3   4   5   6   7   8   9   10

14. Perseverance

1   2   3   4   5   6   7   8   9   10

15. Passion in general

1   2   3   4   5   6   7   8   9   10

16. Passion for your job or whatever you do

1   2   3   4   5   6   7   8   9   10

17. Appreciating others

1   2   3   4   5   6   7   8   9   10

18. Heart versus head

1   2   3   4   5   6   7   8   9   10

19. Spirit of charity

1   2   3   4   5   6   7   8   9   10

20. Your will power

1   2   3   4   5   6   7   8   9   10

Having profiled yourself on the above parameters, identify your strengths and weaknesses and make a sincere effort to improve upon your shortcomings. Also remember, that you have some strengths. Be proud of them and use them effectively in your day-to-day life to live better than before.

The Winning Edge . . .

"A two-day workshop on Emotional Competencies and transition to success"

This two-day workshop conducted by Virender Kapoor who is a thinker, a practitioner, a management Guru and a motivational Maverick with a new mantra is meant for all those who want to bring in a change to themselves. A change for better productivity for organizations as well as individuals.

Purpose and objective of this workshop.

This two-day interactive thought provoking and action inducing session aims to bring out the winner in you. It shows you how to explore your own potential leverage on your strengths, work on your shortfalls and move towards ultimate success.

This is a very powerful programme, which will act like a lifetime inoculation for sustainable motivation and high-end leadership. With "value based leadership" and "value based motivation" at its very core it will change the attitude of participants at a much deeper level.

Attrition and Job hopping is the biggest corporate money buster today. This programme discusses innovative ways to retain people. This workshop motivates participants towards organisational committment, trust and sense of belonging.

You will rejuvenate, reinvent and rediscover yourself. *This programme takes you beyond motivation.*

Workshop Highlights

- Your strengths and weaknesses – rediscover yourself.
- Links your emotions to motivation.
- Your temperament – beyond the "attitude".
- Social competence and handling people.
- Leaders and mentors – changing styles and roles.
- Organisational culture – how to retain people.
- Understanding and controlling emotional responses – applied emotional intelligence.
- The four P's of Ultimate Success.

For more details visit: www.virenderkapoor.com

Contact for Public and In-house Programmes:
virenderkapoor@rediffmail.com
virenderkapoor@vsnl.net
workshop@virenderkapoor.com

What the Participants have to say about Virender Kapoor's Workshop – "The Winning Edge . . ."

"Now I truly possess The Winning Edge."

Rajeev Thakkar, *Kotak Mahindra Mutual Fund*

"I am feeling great by attending this workshop as it was interactive, participative and has given a new dimension to my professional career and personal life."

Sanjay Tripathy, *Sterlite Industries India – Vedanta Group*

"It is a mind opener!"

V. Prabhakaran, *BSNL*

"A programme that sets your mind thinking about whether your heart is in the right place!!!"

Vinayak Joshi, *Airtel*

"Extremely useful and time well spent."

M.A. Jaideep, *Voice and Data*

"A very enriching experience, in fact an eye opener to the changing cultures!"

Mamta Prabhu, *BPL Mobile Cellular Ltd.*

"Very meaningful, soul searching experience of 2 days . . . . Helped to revisit my mission of life within individual capacities/skill sets with utmost respect to human values and emotions."

Harsh Das, *Tata Indicom*

"Biggest gain without any pain."

Sanjay Sehgal, *D-Link (India) Ltd.*

"Simply a terrific feeling!"

Deepak Ramesh, *Tata Indicom*

"It was a great experience!.

Ravindra Nath D, *Sterlite Optical Technologies Ltd.*

"It has changed my "Nazaria" towards life."

S. Sanjit Bhatia, *Sterlite Optical Technologies Ltd.*

"The program has given me a thorough opportunity to re-look at all aspects of life ranging from "womb to tomb.""

Ajay Sukhatankar, *BPL Mobile Cellular Ltd.*

"Probably the best session I have attended on Soft Skills."

Ashish Arora, *Kanbay*

"There were many questions in my mind and it has answered most of them."

Vijay Raghvan, *Kanbay*

"It has set me seriously thinking about what is "My cup of Tea". Beyond that, I have some very useful pointers on managing emotions and patterns of leadership. The whole area of Emotional Intelligent was very well dealt with."

Iishwar Dass Nair, *Cyber Media*

"You have kindled our thoughts. Now its up to me to sit back once in a while introspect, and make myself HAPPY!"

Vinod Gadiyaran, *BPL Mobile Cellular Ltd.*

"Inspiring and Thought Provoking."

Vinod V, *Kotak Mahindra Ltd.*

"Review of my own Management Style."

Virinder Khosla, *Saint-Gobain Ltd.*

"The program is "ENLIGHTENING.""

Aniruddh Basu, *Idea Cellular Ltd.*

"The workshop –"The Winning Edge" is very useful and much beyond my expectations for building competence and success."

S.K. Adak, *BSNL*

"The two-day workshop was very enlightening and thought provoking!"

Esha K, *Airtel*

"Kick-off session for my sleeping ambitions"

Mehul Gajjar, *Amul Dairy*

"Eye opener for the heart and head."

Sudheer Sudhakaran, *Amul Diary*

"Promise to make your life, achieve your destiny and bring smile on the millions of faces."

Vaibhav Trivedi, *Karvy Consultants Ltd.*

"You cannot succeed in life, without the involvement of or listening to your heart, which pumps in the necessary blood of human values, ethics throughout the body.

Parag Palsapure, *Qualcomm India Pvt.Ltd*

"Brought out the Latent strengths within us."

Sanjeev Mondra, *ICICI OneSource*

"The Emotional Competence – A Perspective of Life."

Samir Nayak, *Titan Industries Ltd.*

"This workshop has conveyed that if we can channelize our emotions we can be a winner. Emotions Intelligence can be a Force Multiplier."

Deepak Saxena, *Qualcomm India Pvt.Ltd*

"Heart Over Matter: This course taught me how to become a good human being."

Amelendu Mahapatra, *Nelco Limited*

"The Winning Edge has awakened my latent emotions on how to live a better life."

Faradaz Hafizjee, *ZTE Corporation*